D1117288

GIANTS!
GIANTS!
GIANTS!

GIANTS!
GIANTS!
GIANTS!

From Many Lands and Many Times

Selected by

Helen Hoke

Illustrated by

Stephen Lavis

Franklin Watts
New York/London/Toronto/Sydney/1980

Library of Congress Cataloging in Publication Data
Main entry under title:
Giants! Giants! Giants!
(Terrific triple)
SUMMARY: A selection of 14 stories and 2 poems all
relating to folk and fictional giants.
1. Tales. 2. Giants (in religion, folklore, etc.)
[1. Folklore. 2. Giants—Fiction]   I. Hoke, Helen,
1903-   II. Lavis, Stephen.   III. Series.
PZ8.1.G356   398.2′1   80-10599
ISBN 0-531-04172-7

Contents

Acknowledgments

The selections in this book are used by permission of and special arrangements with the proprietors of their respective copyrights, who are listed below. The editor's and publisher's thanks go to all who made this collection possible.

The editor and publisher have made every effort to trace ownership of all material contained herein. It is their belief that the necessary permissions from publishers, authors, and authorized agents have been obtained in all cases. In the event of any questions arising as to the use of any material, the editor and publisher express regret for any error unconsciously made and will be pleased to make the necessary correction in future editions of the book.

"The Boy Who Overcame the Giants" by Cyrus Macmillan. Reprinted from *Canadian Wonder Tales* by Cyrus Macmillan by permission of The Bodley Head.

"David and Goliath" by Walter de la Mare. Reprinted by permission of the Literary Trustees of Walter de la Mare and The Society of Authors as their representative.

"Finlay, the Giant Killer" from *The Double Knights* by James McNeill. © Oxford University Press, Canada. Copyright © 1965 by the author. Reprinted by permission of Henry Z. Walck, Inc., a division of the David McKay Co.

"The Giant and his Swing" from *Myths and Legends of Fiji* by A. W. Reed and Inez Hames (A.H. and A.W. Reed Ltd., Wellington, New Zealand).

"The Giant and the Pygmies" by Roger Lancelyn Green, from *Stories of Ancient Greece*. Reproduced by permission of The Hamlyn Publishing Group Ltd.

About this Book

Psychic phenomena may not seem very real unless you have experienced some disquieting or possibly comforting manifestation of an unfamiliar power. Stories of ghostly visitors from the past may be unnerving yet not entirely credible. Science fiction may seem more a product of bizarre imaginations than a realistic prediction of what could happen to the inhabitants of this planet within the next few decades.

On the other hand, you may never have seen a giant but you cannot deny the existence of such a species. There is too much scientifically acceptable evidence in the numerous human skeletons of huge proportions discovered by archaeologists. There was even a Regiment of Giants in Prussia around the turn of the seventeenth century.

The myths and legends of most countries throughout the world not surprisingly include stories of the exploits of these demigods of the folklore of their varied homelands. They may have different characteristics. The giant trolls of Scandinavia must be concealed by daybreak or the sunlight turns them into stone forever. The spirits who haunt the abandoned tin mines of south-west England are said to be ghosts of Cornish giants; though usually very small and ugly, they are capable of swelling to an enormous size. Not all giants were ogres: sometimes their feats revealed superhuman strength rather than brutality.

Such folk tales have flourished through the ages, largely due to the strong tradition of story telling in communities solely dependent on such entertainment. Most national myths have therefore developed slowly, but in the United States the process

9

has been necessarily compressed into the span of just a few generations. Undoubtedly the most famous figure in American folklore is Paul Bunyan who is now more widely known than when he was the hero of the logging camps in the last century. Wherever the lumberjacks went across the American continent—from Maine to Oregon—they took with them tales of his exploits. Distinguished American writers like W. H. Auden, Robert Frost and Louis Untermeyer have all used Paul Bunyan as a subject, with the shared intention of ensuring that his legend should be recognized as a pillar of the national folk tradition.

In choosing the stories for this collection I have tried to emphasize how the versatile powers of these gigantic figures affected ordinary people. I hope you will enjoy meeting this galaxy of giants who once dominated their particular territories.

Helen Hoke

Paul Bunyan and his Great Blue Ox

Retold by Wallace Wadsworth

The legend of Paul Bunyan embodies the souls of the millions of American men who did the hard and perilous pioneer work in the early days of settlement camps.

The legend has its origin in the Papineau Rebellion of 1837, when the French-Canadians revolted against their British queen. In the Two Mountains country, many loggers armed with mattocks, axes and wooden forks stormed into battle, and among them was a mighty-muscled bearded giant named Paul Bunyan. He came out of the rebellion with great fame among his own kind and his slaughters received the grandeur of legend.

Later, this heroic young man operated a logging camp, and in those days logging was very hard work indeed. It was the American loggers who made Paul Bunyan a true hero of the evening entertainment in camp. They gave him Babe, the Great Blue Ox, and created the wonderful mythical logging camp. They made Paul Bunyan an inventor and orator, and an industrialist whose efforts surpassed even those of Hercules. He ruled American life in the period between the Winter of the Blue Snow and the Spring That the Rain Came Up From China. By 1860, Paul Bunyan had become a genuine American legendary hero, who visualized perfectly American love of tall talk and tall doings; the true American exuberance and flamboyance.

Legend has it that Paul was born in a town on the coast of Maine. As a child he quickly grew to such an enormous size and strength that his parents

11

were forced to move into the wilderness to find enough room for him to grow. In the wilderness Paul learned his father's trade as a logger and acquired a wife almost as big and strong as himself. Together with Babe, the Great Blue Ox, they happily returned to live in the town of his origin.

So here Paul came, once more nearing the town where he had been born. A giant figure of a fellow now, he pushed his way through the thick timber, bending aside the trees in his road as if they were stalks of grass. Following closely at his heels was Babe, with Mrs. Paul perched on his back, and Jim, the pet crow, comfortably riding on Babe's left horn. They finally came out of the woods into a clearing, and there Paul decided to camp.

It so happened that a hunter stepped into the opposite side of the clearing just about the time that Paul and his companions appeared from among the trees. Unnoticed by the newcomers, he stood for a moment, gazing spellbound at what he saw. Then, with all the haste that he could muster, he sneaked back along the path that he had come and ran with all speed towards town.

Breathlessly he burst upon the crowd of loafers before old Deacon White's store and told what he had seen. "I tell you I saw it myself!" he shouted angrily as his listeners laughed in disbelief. "There he was, a great tall man that would make ten of any of you—yes, more than ten! Brushed trees out of his way like grass, he did, and he had an ox with him that's as big as any forty oxen around these parts. A *blue* ox, at that, as blue as indigo! And if you don't believe me, you can go look for yourselves," with which defiance he stared around at his listeners in a high and mighty manner, proud of being the centre of interest.

12

Deacon White, a very old man who was certainly the richest and shrewdest person in all the country around, had listened with interest to the hunter's story. "Um-m, well," he offered, "mebbe it's Paul Bunyan come home again. I don't calc'late it could be anyone else."

"And furthermore," he went on, glancing with contempt at the men before him, "if that's who it is, mebbe I can get him to log off that deestrict of mine back in the hills that none of you timid woodsmen will touch." With a snort of derision he turned his back on them and gave orders for his chore boy to saddle his horse at once. As soon as he was mounted, he lost no time in galloping towards the clearing where the stranger was reported to be.

"Hallo, there," piped the Deacon, when he was finally in sight of the camp. "Be you Paul Bunyan?"

"That's my name!" Paul answered, bending low over the old man so that he could hear him better. He was very much pleased that someone remembered him after all the years he had been away.

"I thought so," explained the other. "I'm Deacon White. Lived in these parts a long time, I have. Knew your pappy and mammy, and knew you when you were a baby. He-he!" and the old man's white whiskers shook as he chuckled over certain memories. "You raised quite a ruckus around here then—don't reckon I'll ever forget all the excitement you stirred up," and the old man chuckled again.

Paul's gratification was beginning to turn to embarrassment when his visitor finally made his errand known.

"You showed so much promise as a youngster," said the Deacon, "that now I've come to offer you a good job of hard work that no one else is man enough to tackle."

"Bully for you!" responded Paul heartily. "That's just what I'm looking for. What is it?" Prospects of a difficult task

13

interested him at once, for along with the great strength that Nature had given him, he had developed a passion for using that strength in the hardest kind of labour. It seemed a privilege for him to be able to do the grand and thrilling work of the woods. In fact, during his years as lumberman, whenever he found his men soldiering or loafing on the job—as sometimes happened once or twice a season when cabin fever infected them—he would send them all back to camp to think over their shame and joyfully do all their tasks by himself. So now he listened to what the Deacon had to offer. "If it has to do with the woods, and if it's worthwhile, I'm your man," he promised.

"It's all of that," the old man told him. "Back in the mountains I have several thousand sections of fine timber that has never been touched by an axe. I need these logs for my mills, but I can't get any of these half-portion lumbermen around here to log off the tract for me. It's said that there are a lot of Agropelters and Gumberoos there, and mebbe other critters as well, and they have scared every one else out so that they are afraid to go into those woods.

"I don't calc'late they could run you out, though, could they?" and he peered up at the giant form before him with such an amusing, quizzical look that Paul burst into a roar of laughter so loud that the old Deacon was thrown from his horse and the people back in town thought it was thundering.

Now Gumberoos and Agropelters were, in the early days, a very real danger to woodsmen, and any tract of timberland that sheltered them was rightly shunned by all ordinary persons. Most people today have never heard of them, having forgotten that long years ago, before most of the forests were cut down, there were a lot of queer animals living in the wild places where men seldom ventured.

Most of these animals are now extinct because the lumbermen have destroyed their hiding places, but in the early days they

14

were to be found here and there and some of them were very dangerous to man. There were the Ring-Tailed Bavalorous and the Whintosser, for instance, the Agropelter and the Gumberoo, the Snoligoster, and a lot of others. At one time and another, as history shows, Paul Bunyan met up with quite a few of them during his logging operations.

The Agropelter was a very strange animal, and was greatly feared because he had a special hatred for all mankind. No woodsman was ever anxious to run across him. He was very strong, with a slender, wiry body, a villainous ape-like face, and long thin arms like muscular whip-lashes, so powerful that they could break off dead branches and hurl them with the force of a cannon ball.

The Agropelter liked to tuck himself away in the hollow of a dead and rotted tree, and there lie in wait for his enemy, man, to come by. When a luckless human being happened to pass beneath his den, the Agropelter would seize a large club which he kept handy for the purpose, and with his whip-like arms would hurl it with such unerring aim that very seldom did he fail to crack the skull of the unlucky intruder. The animal fed only upon hootowls and woodpeckers, and the toughness of his diet, together with its scarcity, is thought to have been the cause of his continuous rage.

The Gumberoo was a truly fearsome creature that infested various stretches of woodland. He was almost round in shape, and was the largest animal in the woods. He was safe from all enemies because of his skin, which was like leather and so thick nothing could pierce it. He could eat a horse at one meal, and had been known to destroy a whole herd of moose without the least injury from the terrible horns of the fierce bulls. In fact, no creature was ever able to find a vulnerable spot in the animal's anatomy, for whatever struck the beast bounced off again with the same force. Even when a rifle was fired at him, so tough was his hide and so elastic his body, that the bullet was sure to bounce back at exactly the same speed and strike the hunter squarely between the eyes. He was always hungry, always ready to eat anything that looked like food, and was especially fond of human beings.

There was one thing, however, which the Gumberoo greatly feared, which he had no protection against, and that was fire. He was of a very inflammable nature, burning like celluloid if fire ever touched him and finally blowing up with the tremendous force of gun powder. Woodsmen claim that occasionally the creatures could be heard exploding with loud reports when they happened to get caught in forest fires, and it is thought that the increasing prevalence of such fires has had much to do with their scarcity of recent years. So fearful of fire were they that just the smell of smoke would drive them away, and it was through knowledge of this weakness that Paul and his men eventually cleared the Deacon's woods of these fierce creatures.

So it was not very strange that the Deacon could find no one willing to log off timberlands where Agropelters and Gumberoos were lying in wait. Paul Bunyan, however, was quite different from other men, and he just laughed at the danger. "I'm your man, Deacon," he promised, and they at once began discussing terms.

When they had come to an agreement, Paul said, "You draw up the papers, Deacon, and arrange for the necessary supplies of grub and tools and other things. I'll strike out for the woods at once, pick a location for my camp, and start getting my crew together. It'll soon be late fall now, and I want to start cutting by the time the first snow comes. Are there any men in town that I might have use for?"

The old man snorted in disgust. "All pretty poor stuff, except Swedish Ole, the blacksmith," he replied. "He's the biggest man around here, though not so big as you. When he puts shoes on a

16

horse he takes the animal up on his lap like a baby. He's a mighty good blacksmith, all right, but I expect folks will be glad to get him out of town, as he's kind of clumsy and they're all afraid of getting stepped on sometime."

"I'll need a smith, and he sounds like a good man," said Paul. "You sign him up for me, and he can join me later. Meanwhile, I'll get busy, as I have said, and will manage to see you again before long." So, after making further arrangments for his wife to accompany the Deacon back to town, where she was to remain while he was in the woods, Paul started away, followed by Babe, the Great Blue Ox.

He travelled many miles through the forest and over mountains, and figured that he must be getting near the Deacon's tract of woodland. Then all at once he began to hear sounds like long peals of near-by thunder. He looked at the sky, and saw that the sun was setting perfectly clear, with not a cloud to be seen, so he knew there could be no storm coming up. As he went on the sounds grew louder, and Paul became more puzzled than ever. Finally he came out into a cleared space on the side of a mountain where a forest fire had swept the slope clean of trees from bottom to top, and there he saw a very strange thing.

Hearing the thundering noise again, he looked ahead, and was surprised to see a great round stone as big as a house rolling down the mountainside towards the valley below. It came bounding along at great speed, gaining momentum with every turn, and as it rolled along it jarred the earth with the thunderous sounds he had been hearing. But strangest of all was the man who was running along beside it, holding something tightly against it as it turned over and over. Paul looked more closely, and saw other stones rolling downhill in the same manner, and along with each one, keeping pace with it, was a tall, strongly built man with something in his hand. "I wonder what queer new game they are playing," Paul said to himself,

17

walking on to get a nearer view.

Then it was that he began to understand what the men were doing. Each of them had an axe in his hand, and was holding its edge to the stone as it turned over and over in its headlong flight down the steep slope. The men were grinding their axes!

Thus it was that Paul Bunyan caught first sight of the Seven Axemen, mighty men of the woods, whose heroic fame through later years was almost as great as his own. These men were with him through most of his lumbering operations, and for many years they continued to sharpen their axes in this way, starting a huge round stone rolling down a long steep hill and running along beside it holding the edge of an axe to it as it turned.

Later, when they moved with Paul to the Dakotas they had no hills steep or long enough to serve their purpose, and it was then that Paul invented the revolving grindstone so common today, to take the place of the rolling rocks. But that was a later development.

The Seven Axemen! Noble figures they were, never equalled before or since, except by Paul Bunyan himself. They were cousins, it is said, and came originally from Canada. Each could cut down several square miles of timber in a day without exerting himself, and then not be too tired afterwards to join in the pranks and horseplay of the camp. They were jolly fellows, and Paul got along with them through many years.

On this first day of their meeting, observing that they had company, the Axemen dropped their labours and came forward to greet the newcomer, all happy at having a visitor. They were congenial lads, with hearts as big as their two fists, and they welcomed Paul with great friendliness. They cast many admiring glances at his great size and at the hugeness of Babe, the Blue Ox, as one can well imagine, though they were almost as big as Paul themselves. With the greatest hospitality, they invited him

18

to stay overnight with them, and so, just as the sun had set, they all presently came to the big log shanty where the Seven Axemen lived.

After their tools had been put away, their visitor accompanied them to the little lake nearby where they proceeded to wash before supper, and such a splashing did the lot of them make that they just plain splashed all the water out of the lake so that it was never of any use after that. Just then the supper horn blew, and they tramped back and into the shanty.

There Paul met the Little Chore Boy—a youngster who did the cooking, attended to the chores, and did all the light work that had to be done—while the Seven Axemen attended to all the heavy labour. As the Little Chore Boy weighed only eight hundred pounds, he had to put up with a great deal of joshing and teasing from the Seven Axemen because of his small size.

They all sat down to supper except the Little Chore Boy, whose duty it was to wait on them and who never sat down to table with full-grown men. Such a supper it was! The Little Chore Boy was continually groaning under the weight of the food he carried to the table. The Seven Axemen were hearty eaters—a half of a full-grown hog was only a slice of bacon to them—and Paul's appetite was so much greater even than theirs that he immediately won the deep admiration of them all.

Finally the toothpicks were passed, and everybody sat back and began to fill his pipe. Paul had been wondering what the cord of firewood was on the table for, until he found out that the Seven Axemen used cordwood for toothpicks. When all had their pipes going, they moved away from the table to give the Little Chore Boy a chance to clean up.

Paul had never found anyone he liked so well as he did these Seven Axemen. He could see that they were all good lumbermen, too, well acquainted with the work of logging of timber and accustomed to doing everything in a big way, and so he started to tell them about the contract he had made to log the Deacon's tract.

They were greatly interested, nor did they hesitate in giving him an answer when he offered them top places on his crew. They liked hard work—the harder the job the better they liked it—and to work for such a mighty man as Paul Bunyan appealed to them very strongly. They accepted his offer, there and then.

Afterwards, everybody being greatly pleased over the new arrangements, they lounged before the fire and sang *Bung Yer Eye* and *Shanty Boy* until the people back along the coast miles away thought a storm was blowing up.

Paul's first task, after he and the Seven Axemen had finally come to the place in the Deacon's woods where he intended to build his camp, was to get rid of the Gumberoos and Agropelters. So while the Axemen seated themselves, leaned their backs comfortably against broad tree trunks and lit their pipes, Paul stood thinking out some method of driving the troublesome creatures away. Paul was a great thinker, and there was never any problem that could keep him puzzled long.

"The Gumberoos are afraid of fire," he said to himself, "and they will run away if they notice even the least sign of it. Now that is a weakness that I ought to be able to use against them—but how?" and he thought so hard over the matter that the Seven Axemen could hear the low whir of his brain working. Just then a big cloud of smoke from one of the Axemen's pipes floated up and encircled Paul's head, and when he finally stopped coughing and had caught his breath again a look of great satisfaction spread over his face. He had figured out a way to drive the Gumberoos away.

"I want you bullies to rest up for a few days," he said to the Seven Axemen, and there was a twinkle in his eyes. "There's plenty of hard work on the job ahead, but I'm not quite ready for you to start on it yet. So just you sit around and take things easy for a while, until I am ready for you to begin," and he tossed down his big tobacco pouch where all could reach it and sauntered away.

The Seven Axemen looked at one another and grinned, and then they proceeded to fill up their pipes again. If their new boss wanted to pay them their wages just for loafing, why, they were perfectly willing to accommodate him. They had often looked forward to such a time as this, when they might take their ease and talk and smoke together, all without being worried by the thought that they were leaving necessary tasks undone or were losing valuable working time. Never before had the opportunity of indulging in such fancied leisure come to them, and now they settled back to enjoy themselves to the fullest extent.

Many were the subjects which they discussed and great the problems which they settled. Countless were the tales of woodland adventure which they told, and mighty were the labours each performed in the telling. Oh, wonderful men, those Seven Axemen—wonderful in brain as well as in muscle. So tireless were their minds that they could listen to the same joke a hundred times a day, and laugh each time harder than the last.

And all the time while they rested they smoked their pipes, wonderful old pipes which they had used constantly through many, many years. Each one used up two bushels of tobacco every time it was filled, and by the time the second day had come to an end the contents of Paul's tobacco pouch were almost half gone. The smoke hung over the land like a cloud, and for hundreds of miles there was not a Gumberoo to be found in the woods.

The fierce creatures, sniffing the strangling smoke which filled the air, had been fooled into thinking that a terrible fire was raging through the forest. Frightened nearly out of their wits, they had scrambled away as fast as they could roll. No one knows how far they went, for they were never seen nor heard of again in that part of the country.

Getting rid of the Agropelters was the next task, and this required a little more work. Paul called the Seven Axemen to him, and they were very glad to put away their pipes and gather around him. They had smoked so much that their tongues were sore, and their two-day rest had grown so tiresome that they were anxious to get back to hard work again.

"These Agropelters all hide away in the hollows of dead trees," Paul told them. "Now I want you to get your axes and wander through the timber. Every time you see a dead tree, or one with a hollow in it, chop it down and split it open. After you have done that, we'll start putting up the camp."

With a whoop, the Seven Axemen set about the task as if it were a game. Being so large and strong, they had no fear of the animals, and as one blow from their great axes was usually enough to smash even the biggest hollow tree into splinters, they worked fast. It was only a day or so before there was not a hollow tree to be found standing in all the Deacon's timberland, and with their hiding places all gone, the Agropelters also fled far away.

Paul was very much pleased that the woods were now safe for ordinary men, and he praised the Seven Axemen highly for their work. He set them to putting up bunkhouses and stables and the cook shanty, for the new camp, and he ordered the Little Chore Boy to carry the word far and near that now, since the dangerous animals were all driven out of the woods, he would be giving high pay that winter to all good loggers who cared to join his crew.

Men soon began drifting into camp from every direction, and Paul hired all the best ones. A man had to be extra good to get a job with Paul Bunyan, but even so it wasn't so very long before he had gathered together as sturdy a bunch of woodsmen as has ever been seen.

It was about this time that he made a trip back to town, where he saw the Deacon again and arranged all the little matters that were so far unsettled regarding the work, and when he started on his return trip to camp he was accompanied by Ole, the smith. Ole, or the Big Swede, as he was quite often called, was a slow-witted but amiable chap whose mind could never hold more than one idea at a time. He was gigantic in size—though not as big as Paul—and was a past master in all that had to do with his trade of metal-working. From the first, he regarded Paul with a liking that was almost worship, and next to Paul in his affections came Paul's great helper, Babe, the Great Blue Ox. Indeed, so remarkable was his admiration for the magnificent animal that Paul at once turned over to him the duty of caring for Babe, which task he gladly accepted and continued to perform through many years.

Paul had taken the Blue Ox with him to town, and there he loaded him with all the supplies that would be needed for the camp and crew during the winter. When everything had been packed on Babe's back, the animal was so heavily laden that on the way back to camp he sank to his knees in the solid rock at nearly every step. These footprints later filled with water and became the countless lakes which are to be found today scattered throughout the state of Maine.

Babe was compelled to go slowly, of course, on account of the great load he carried, and so Paul had to camp overnight along the way. He took the packs from the Ox's back, turned the big animal out to graze, and after eating supper he and Ole lay down to sleep.

The Blue Ox, however, was for some strange reason in a restless mood that night, and after feeding all that he cared to, he wandered away for many miles before he finally found a place that suited his particular idea of what a bedding ground should be. There he lay down, and it is quite possible that he was very much amused in thinking of the trouble which his master would have in finding him the next morning. The Ox was a very wise creature, and every now and then he liked to play a mischievous little joke on Paul.

Along about dawn Paul Bunyan awoke and looked about for his pet. Not a glimpse of him could he get in any direction, though he whistled so loudly for him that nearby trees were shattered into bits. At last, after he and Ole had eaten their breakfast and Babe still did not appear, Paul knew that the joke was on him. "He thinks he has played a little trick on me," he said to Ole with a grin. "You go ahead and make up the packs again, while I play hide-and-seek for a while," and as the Big Swede started gathering everything together again Paul set off trailing the missing animal.

Babe's tracks were so large that it took three men, standing close together, to see across one of them, and the footprints were so far apart that no one could follow them but Paul, who was such an expert trailer that no one else could ever equal him in this ability. So remarkable was he in this respect that he could follow any tracks that were ever made, no matter how old or how faint they were. It is told of him that he once came across the carcass of a bull moose that had died of old age, and having a couple of hours to spare, and being also of an inquiring turn of mind, he followed the tracks of the moose back to the place where it had been born.

Being such an expert, therefore, it did not take him very long to locate Babe. The Great Blue Ox, when Paul at last came across him, was lying down contentedly chewing his cud, and waiting for his master to come and find him. "You worthless critter!" Paul said to him, and thwacked him good-naturedly with his hand. "Look at the trouble you have put me to, and just look at the damage you have done here." And he pointed to the great hollow place in the ground which Babe had wallowed out

25

while lying there. The Ox's only reply was to smother Paul for a moment with a loving, juicy lick of his great tongue, and then together they set off to where Ole was waiting for them.

Anyone, by looking at a map of the state of Maine, can easily locate Moosehead Lake, which is, as history shows, the place where the Great Blue Ox lay down.

By the time that Paul, Ole and Babe arrived at the logging camp, the first snow had begun to fall, and Paul began to work in earnest. He organized his crew so that each gang of men had a certain task to do, and the rules he developed here and used in his later logging operations have been followed more or less in all lumber camps ever since.

For instance, in the Great Lakes states, where the lumber industry probably reached its highest development, the work of the average logging crew was done much in this way: A gang of choppers would first go through the woods clearing the way. After them would come the sawyers, one man carrying an axe for marking the direction of each tree's fall and a wedge to use if necessary in guiding it, while two others would fell the tree with a crosscut saw. (Paul was the inventor of the two-man saw used in logging, and Ole made up a number from his plans for use in his camps.) The saw having done its work, as the tree began to topple the sawyers would get back out of the way, giving a loud yell, "Timber-r!" as a warning to anyone else nearby, and the great trunk would come swishing and crashing to the ground.

Then would come the scaler, who would measure the fallen trees into proper log lengths, and the sawyers would cut them at his marks. Next, the skidding crew or swamper would clear the way for the teamsters, who would drag or haul the logs to the stagings by the stream. Winter was always best for logging, for then the logs could be easily skidded over roads which they made slippery by sprinkling water on them until they were paved with hard and solid ice.

26

At the stream the deckers would pile the logs on the skidways, from which, in the spring when the freshets filled the stream with swift water, they would be dumped to float down-river on the big drive. When the time of the drive came, the entire crew would join in following it, riding the logs with calked boots and carrying pikepole or peavy, fighting jams and snaking stranded logs off the banks all along the way. When the logs finally reached the booms of the sawmill towards which they were headed, the logger's work was over, and he usually celebrated the ending of the drive in a grand and glorious manner, fighting out old grudges accumulated during the winter and otherwise enjoying himself.

That is something of the way a logging crew usually works and lives. Of course, Paul had the help of the remarkable Babe, and of such mighty woodsmen as the Seven Axemen, and he did things in his own peculiar way which no one else could hope to imitate. In the main, however, the camps of later years were organized much after the fashion that he established.

No one, certainly, could be expected to copy Paul in the matter of straightening out crooked logging trails. It was all wild country where Paul did his logging, and about the only roads which he found through the woods were the trails and paths made by the wild animals that had travelled over them for hundreds of years.

Paul decided to use these game trails as logging roads, but they twisted and turned in every direction and were all so crooked that they had to be straightened before any satisfactory use could be made of them. It is well known that the Great Blue Ox was so powerful that he could pull anything that had two ends, and so when Paul wanted a crooked logging trail straightened out, he would just hitch Babe up to one end of it, tell his pet to go ahead, and, lo and behold! the crooked trail would be pulled out perfectly straight.

There was one particularly bad stretch of road, about twenty or thirty miles long, that gave Babe and Paul a lot of trouble before they finally got all the crooks pulled out of it. It certainly must have been the crookedest road in the world—it twisted and turned so much that it spelled out every letter of the alphabet, some of the letters two or three times. Paul taught Babe the letters of the alphabet, just by leading him over it a few times, and men going along it met themselves coming from the other direction so often that the whole camp was near crazy before long.

So Paul decided that the road would have to be straightened out without any further delay, and with that end in view he ordered Ole to make for him the strongest chain he knew how. The Big Swede set to work with a will, and when the chain was completed it had links four feet long and two feet across and the steel they were made of was thirteen inches thick.

The chain being ready, Paul hitched Babe up to one end of the road with it. At his master's word the Great Blue Ox began to puff and pull and strain away as he had never done before, and at last he got the end pulled out a little way. Paul spoke to him again, and he pulled harder than ever. With every tug he made one of the twists in the road would straighten out, and then Babe would pull away again, hind legs straight out behind and belly to the ground. It was the hardest job Babe had ever been put up against, but he stuck to it most admirably.

When the task was finally done the Ox was nearly fagged out—a condition that he had never known before—and that big chain had been pulled on so hard that it was pulled out into a solid steel bar. The road was straightened out, however, which was the thing Paul wanted, and he considered the time and energy expended as well worthwhile, since the nuisance had been transformed into something useful. Paul found, though, that since all the kinks and twists had been pulled out, there was now a whole lot more of the road than was needed, but—never being a person who could stand to waste anything which might be useful—he rolled up all the extra length and laid it down in a place where there had never been a road before but where one might come in handy sometime.

Nor was the straightening of crooked roads the only useful work which the Great Blue Ox did. It was also his task to skid or drag the logs from the stumps to the rollways by the streams, where they were stored for the drives. Babe was always obedient, and a tireless and patient worker. It is well remembered that the timber of nineteen states, except a few scant sections here and there which Paul Bunyan did not touch, was skidded from the stumps by the all-powerful Great Blue Ox. He was docile and willing, and could be depended upon for the performance of almost any task set him, except that once in a while he would develop a sudden streak of mischief, and drink a river dry behind a drive or run off into the woods. Sometimes he would step on a ridge that formed the bank of the river, and smash it down so that the river would start running out through his tracks, thus changing its course entirely from what Paul had counted on.

The cutting of the Deacon's timber tract went ahead so fast that Paul began looking ahead and wondering what he would do next. He was very much gratified to find that his fame had already begun to spread, so that he was offered enough logging contracts to keep him busy in that section of the country for several years to come. He was never one to shirk a task, was Paul, and the assurance of having ahead of him all the work that he could do, and Babe as helper, made him happy indeed.

How We Logged Katahdin Stream

(Anonymous)

Come all ye river-drivers, if a tale you wish to hear
The likes for strength and daring all the North Woods has no
    peer:
'Twas the summer of 1860 when we took a brave ox team
And a grand bully band of braggarts up to log Katahdin Stream.

Chorus:
    So, it's Hi derry, Ho derry, Hi derry, Down!
    When our driving is over we'll come into town!
    Make ready, ye maidens, for frolic and song!
    When the woodsman has whiskey, then naught can go wrong!

Bold Gattigan was foreman, he's the pride of Bangor's Town,
And there was no other like Chauncey for to mow the great pines
    down;
Joe Murphraw was the swamper, with Canada Jacques Dupree.
We'd the best camp cook in the wilderness—I know, for it was
    me.

30

We left from Millinocket on such a misty day
We dulled our axes chopping the fog to clear ourselves a way,
Till at last we reached the bottom of Mount Katahdin's peaks
supreme
And vowed that we within the week would clear Katahdin
Stream.

O, Chauncey chopped and Murph he swamped and Canada
Jacques did swear,
Bold Gattigan goaded the oxen on and shouted and tore his hair,
Till the wildwood rang with "Timber!" as the forest monarchs
fell,
And the air was split with echoes of our axe-blows and our yell.

For six whole days and twenty-three hours we threshed the forest
clean—
The logs we skidded by hundreds, O, such a drive was never
seen!
We worked clear round the mountain, and rejoiced to a jovial
strain,
When what did we see but that forest of trees was a-growing in
again!

Then all of a sudden the mountain heaved, and thunder spoke
out of earth!
"Who's walking around in my beard?" it cried, and it rumbled
as though in mirth.
The next we knew, a hand appeared—no larger than Moosehead
Lake—
And it plucked us daintily one by one, while we with fear did
quake!

31

Paul Bunyan held us in one hand! With the other he rubbed his
chin.
"Well I'll be swamped! You fellows have logged my beard right
down to the skin!"
"We thought you was Mount Katahdin," Gattigan shouted into
his ear,
"We're sorry, but 'twouldn't have happened if the weather had
been clear."

Well, good old Paul didn't mind it at all. He paid us for the
shave—
A hundred dollars apiece to the men, to the oxen fodder he gave.
And now, ye young river-drivers, fill your glasses—fill mine
too—
And we'll drink to the health of Bold Gattigan, and his gallant
lumbering crew!

The Boy who Overcame the Giants

A Canadian Indian Story

By Cyrus Macmillan

Giants cannot usually be beaten by strength, but one small boy can overcome three giants if he uses his wits like the boy in this Canadian Indian tale.

Once long ago, before the white man came to Canada, an orphan boy was living alone with his uncle. He was not very happy, for he had to work very hard, and tasks more fitted for a man's shoulders than for a boy's were often placed upon him. When his parents died and left this young boy without brother or sister, his uncle took him to his own home because there was no one else to take care of him.

But the uncle treated him very cruelly and often he wished to get rid of him. It mattered not how well the boy did his work or how many fish and animals he caught, his uncle was never satisfied, and often he beat the boy harshly and with little cause. The boy would have run away but he did not know where to go, and he feared to wander alone in the dark forest. So he decided to endure his hardships as best he could.

Now it happened that in a distant village near the sea there lived a Chief who was noted far and wide for his cruelty. He had a wicked temper, and he was known to have put many people to

34

death for no reason whatsoever. More than all else, he hated boastfulness and he had scanty patience with anyone who was vain of his own strength. He pledged himself always to humble the proud and to debase the haughty. The boy's uncle had heard of this wicked ruler, and he said, "Here is a chance for me to get rid of the boy. I will tell lies about him to the Chief."

It chanced just at this time that three giants came into the Chief's territory. Where they came from, no man knew, but they dwelt in a large cave near the sea, and they caused great havoc and destruction in all the land. They ate up great stores of food, and all the little children they could lay their hands on.

The Chief used every means to get rid of the giants, but without success. Night after night his best warriors went to the cave by the ocean to seek out the giants, but not a man returned. A piece of birch bark bearing a picture of a warrior with an arrow in his heart, found the next day at the Chief's door, always told him of the warrior's fate. And the giants continued their cruel work, for no one could stop them.

Soon all the country was in great terror. The Chief wondered greatly what was to be done. At last he thought, "I will give my daughter to the man who can rid me of these pests." His daughter was his only child and she was very beautiful, and he knew that many suitors would now appear to seek her hand, for although the task was dangerous, the prize was worth while.

When the wicked uncle in the distant village heard of it, he thought, "Now I can get rid of the boy, for I will tell the Chief that the boy says he can kill giants." So, taking his nephew with him, he went to the Chief's house and begged to see him. "Oh, Chief," he said, "I have a boy who boasts that before many days have passed he can free your land from the giants." And the Chief said, "Bring him to me." The man said, "Here he is."

The Chief was surprised when he saw the small boy, and he said, "You have promised that you can rid my land of giants.

35

Now we shall see if you can do it. If you succeed you may have my daughter in marriage. If you fail, you will die. If you escape from the giants, I will kill you myself. I hate vain boasters, and they shall not live in my land."

The boy went and sat by the ocean, and cried as hard as he could. He thought that he would surely die, for he was very small and he had no means of killing the giants. But as he sat there an old woman came along. She came quietly and quickly out of the grey mist of the sea.

"Why are you crying?" she said. And the boy said, "I am crying because I am forced to attack the giants in the cave, and if I cannot kill them I shall surely die," and he cried louder than before.

But the old woman, who was the good fairy of the sea, said, "Take this bag and this knife and these three little stones that I will give you, and when you go to-night to the giants' cave, use them as I tell you and all will be well."

She gave him three small white stones and a small knife, and a bag like the bladder of a bear, and she taught him their use. Then she disappeared into the grey mist that hung low on the ocean and the boy never saw her again.

The boy lay down on the sand and went to sleep. When he awoke, the moon was shining, and far along the coast in the bright light he could see an opening in the rocks which he knew was the entrance to the giants' cave. Taking his bag and his knife and the three little stones, he approached it cautiously with trembling heart.

When he reached the mouth of the cave he could hear the giants snoring inside, all making different noises, louder than the roar of the sea. Then he remembered the old woman's instructions. He tied the bag inside his coat so that the mouth of it was close to his skin. Then he took one of the stones from his pocket. At once it grew to immense size, so heavy that the boy could scarcely hold it. He threw it at the biggest giant with great force, and it hit him squarely on the head.

The giant sat up staring wildly and rubbing his brow. He kicked his younger brother, who was lying beside him, and said in great anger, "Why did you strike me?" "I did not strike you," said his brother. "You struck me on the head while I slept," said the giant, "and if you do it again I will kill you." Then they went to sleep again.

When the boy heard them snoring loudly again, he took a second stone from his pocket. At once it grew great in size and the boy hurled it with great force at the biggest giant. Again the giant sat up staring wildly and rubbing his head. But this time he did not speak. He grasped his axe, which was lying beside him, and killed his brother with a blow. Then he went to sleep again.

When the boy heard him snoring, he took the third stone from his pocket. At once it grew to great size and weight, and he hurled it with all his force at the giant. Again the giant sat up with great staring eyes, rubbing the lump on his head. He was now in a great rage. "My brothers have plotted to kill me," he yelled, and seizing his axe he killed his remaining brother with a blow. Then he went to sleep, and the boy slipped from the cave, first gathering up the three stones, which were now of their usual small size.

The next morning when the giant went to get water from the stream, the boy hid in the trees and began to cry loudly. The giant soon discovered him and asked, "Why are you crying?" "I have lost my way," said the boy, "my parents have gone and left me. Please take me into your service, for I would like to work for such a kind, handsome man, and I can do many things." The giant was flattered by what the boy said, and although he liked to eat little children, he thought, "Now that I am alone, I ought to have a companion, so I will spare the boy's life and make him

37

my servant." And he took the boy back to his cave, and said, "Cook my dinner before I come home. Make some good stew, for I shall be very hungry."

When the giant went into the forest the boy prepared the evening meal. He cut up a great store of deer meat and put it in a large pot bigger than a hogshead, and made a good meat stew.

When the giant came home in the evening he was very hungry, and he was well pleased to see the big pot filled with his favourite food. He seated himself on one side of the pot, and the boy seated himself on the other side, and they dipped their spoons into the big dish. And the boy said, "We must eat it all up so that I can clean the pot well and ready for the corn mush we will have for breakfast."

The stew was very hot, and to cool it before he ate it, the giant blew his breath on what he dipped out. But the boy poured his own share into the bag under his coat, and said, "Why can't you eat hot food—a big man like you? In my country men never stop to cool their stew with their breath."

Now the giant could not see very well, for his eyesight was not very good, and the cave was dark, and he did not notice the boy putting the stew in the bag so quickly. He thought the boy was eating it. And he was shamed by the boy's taunts because he was so much larger than the boy, so he ate up the hot stew at once in great gulps and burned his throat badly. But he was too proud to stop or to complain.

When they had eaten half the potful, the giant said, "I am full. I think I have had enough." "No, indeed," said the boy, "you must show that you *like* my cooking. In my country men eat much more than that," and he kept on eating. The giant was not to be outdone by a boy, so he fell to eating again, and they did not stop until they had consumed the whole potful of stew.

The boy had poured his share into the bag, but when they had finished the giant was swelled out to an immense size. He could

scarcely move, he had eaten so much, and he said, "I have eaten too much; I feel very full, and I have a great pain in my belly." And the boy said, "I do not feel very comfortable myself, but I have a way to cure pains." So saying, he took his little knife and thrust it gently into the side of the bag and the stew oozed out and he was soon back to his normal size. The giant wondered greatly at the sight, but the boy said, "It is a way they have in my country after they have had a great feast."

"Does the knife not hurt?" asked the giant. "No, indeed," said the boy, "it brings great relief." "My throat is very sore," said the giant, for the hot stew had burned him. "You will soon feel better," said the boy, "if you will do as I have done."

The giant hesitated to do this, but soon he felt so uncomfortable that he could bear it no longer. He saw that the boy was feeling quite well. So he took his long knife and plunged it into his stomach. "Strike hard," said the boy, "or it will do you no good." The giant plunged the knife in to the hilt, and in an instant he fell dead.

Then the boy took the stones and the bag and the knife which the Woman of the Mist had given him and went and told the Chief what he had done. The Chief sent his messengers to the cave to make sure that the boy spoke the truth. Sure enough, they found the three giants lying dead.

When they told the Chief what they had seen, he said to the boy "You may have my daughter as your wife." But the boy said, "I do not want your daughter. She is too old and fat. I want only traps to catch fish and game." So the Chief gave the boy many good traps, and he went into a far country to hunt game, and there he lived happily by himself. And his wicked uncle never saw him again.

But the land was troubled no more by giants, because of the boy's great deeds.

The Great Quillow

By James Thurber

The troubled councillors of the small town listened to the town clerk reading the impossible demands made by the powerful giant, Hunder. They knew their limited resources would quickly be exhausted but were cynical about the little toymaker's plan to overthrow their unwelcome visitor.

Once upon a time, in a far country, there lived a giant named Hunder. He was so enormous in height and girth and weight that little waves were set in motion in distant lakes when he walked. His great fingers could wrench a clock from its steeple as easily as a child might remove a peanut from its shell. Every morning he devoured three sheep, a pie made of a thousand apples, and a chocolate as high and as wide as a spinning wheel. It would have taken six ordinary men to lift the great brass key to his front door, and four to carry one of the candles with which he lighted his house.

It was Hunder's way to strip a town of its sheep and apples and chocolate, its leather and cloth, its lumber and tallow and brass, and then move on to a new far village and begin his depredations again. There had been no men strong enough to thwart his evil ways in any of the towns he had set upon and impoverished. He had broken their most formidable weapons between his thumb and forefinger, laughing like the hurricane. And there had been no men cunning enough in any of the towns to bring about his destruction. He had crushed their most

41

ingenious traps with the toe of his mammoth boot, guffawing like a volcano.

One day Hunder strode hundreds and hundreds of leagues and came to a little town in a green valley. It was a staunch little town and a firm little valley, but they quaked with the sound of his coming. The houses were narrow and cobbled. There were not many people in the town: a hundred men, a hundred women, a hundred children.

Every Tuesday night at seven o'clock a council of ten met to administer the simple affairs of the community. The councillors were the most important tradesmen and artisans of New Moon Street, a short, narrow, cobbled street that ran east and west. These men were the tailor, the butcher, the candymaker, the blacksmith, the baker, the candlemaker, the lamplighter, the cobbler, the carpenter, and the locksmith. After the small business of the tranquil town had been taken care of, the council members sat around and speculated as to the number of stars in the sky, discussed the wonderful transparency of glass, and praised the blueness of violets and the whiteness of snow. Then they made a little fun of Quillow, the toymaker (whose work they considered a rather pretty waste of time), and went home.

Quillow, the toymaker, did not belong to the council, but he attended all its meetings. The councilmen were fond of Quillow because of the remarkable toys he made, and because he was a droll and gentle fellow. Quillow made all kinds of familiar playthings on his long and littered workbench: music boxes, jumping jacks, building blocks; but he was famous for a number of little masterpieces of his own invention: a clown who juggled three marbles, a woodman who could actually chop wood, a trumpeter who could play seven notes of a song on a tiny horn, a paperweight in which roses burst into bloom in falling snow.

Quillow was as amusing to look at as any of his toys. He was the shortest man in town, being only five feet tall. His ears were large, his nose was long, his mouth was small, and he had a shock of white hair that stood straight up like a dandelion clock. The lapels of his jacket were wide. He wore a red tie in a deep-pointed collar and his pantaloons were baggy and unpressed. At Christmas time each year Quillow made little hearts of gold for the girls of the town and hearts of oak for the boys. He considered himself something of a civic figure, since he had designed the spouting dolphins in the town fountain, the wooden animals on the town merry-go-round, and the twelve scarlet men who emerged from the dial of the town clock on the stroke of every hour and played a melody on little silver bells with little silver hammers.

It was the custom of Quillow's colleagues to shout merrily, "Why, here comes the Great Quillow!" when the toymaker appeared. The lamplighter or the tailor or the locksmith would sometimes creep up behind him and pretend to wind a key in his back as if he were a mechanical figure of his own devising. Quillow took all this in good part, and always, when the imaginary key in his back was turned, he would walk about stiff-legged, with jerky movements of his arms, joining in the fun and increasing the laughter.

It was different on the day the giant arrived. Laughter was hushed and the people hid in their houses and talked in frightened whispers when Hunder's great bulk appeared like a cyclone in the sky, and the earth shook beneath him. Panting a little after his thousand-league walk, Hunder pulled up four trees from a hillside to make room for his great hulk, and sat down. Hunder surveyed the town and grunted. There was no one to be seen in the streets. Not even a cat crept over the cobblestones.

"Ho, town!" bawled Hunder. The doors shook and the windows rattled. "Ho, town! Send me your clerk that you may hear Hunder's will!"

The town clerk gathered up quill and ink and parchment.

43

"There are ninety-nine other men in town," he grumbled, "but it's the town clerk this, and the town clerk that, and the town clerk everything." He walked out of his house, still grumbling and trudged across the valley to hear the giant's will.

An hour later the town clerk sat at the head of a long table in the council room and began to call the roll. "We're all here," snapped the blacksmith. "You can see that."

The clerk continued with the roll call.

"Baker," he called. "Here," said the baker. "Blacksmith," he droned. "Here," said the blacksmith sourly.

The clerk finished calling the roll and looked over his spectacles. "We have a visitor tonight, as usual," he said, "Quillow, the toymaker. I will make the proper entry in the minutes."

"Never mind the minutes," said the blacksmith. "Read us the demands of Hunder the giant."

The clerk entered Quillow's name in the minutes. "Now," he said, "I will read the minutes of the last meeting."

The candymaker stood up. "Let's dispense with the minutes of the last meeting," he said.

The clerk looked over his spectacles. "It must be properly moved and duly seconded," he said. It was properly moved and duly seconded. "Now read the demands of Hunder the giant," shouted the blacksmith.

The clerk rapped on the table with his gavel. "Next," he said, "comes unfinished business. We have before us a resolution to regulate the speed of merry-go-rounds."

"Dispense with it!" bawled the blacksmith.

"It must be properly moved and duly seconded," said the clerk.

It was properly moved and duly seconded and the clerk at last unrolled a long scroll of parchment. "We come now," he said,

"to the business of the day. I have here the demands of Hunder the giant. The document is most irregular. It does not contain a single 'greeting' or 'whereas' or 'be it known by these presents'!"

Everyone sat motionless as the clerk began to read the scroll.

"I, Hunder, must have three sheep every morning," he read.

"That would use up all the sheep in the valley in a week and a fortnight," said the butcher, "and there would be no mutton for our own people."

"I, Hunder, must have a chocolate a day as high and as wide as a spinning wheel," read the town clerk.

"Why, that would exhaust all the chocolate in my storeroom in three days!" cried the candymaker.

The town clerk read from the parchment again. "I, Hunder, must have a new jerkin made for me in a week and a fortnight."

"Why, I would have to work night and day to make a jerkin in a week and a fortnight for so large a giant," gasped the tailor, "and it would use up all the cloth on my shelves and in my basement."

"I, Hunder," went on the town clerk, "must have a new pair of boots within a week and a fortnight."

The cobbler moaned as he heard this. "Why, I would have to work night and day to make a pair of boots for so large a giant in a week and a fortnight," he said. "And it would use up all the leather in my workshop and in my back room."

The council members shook their heads sadly as each demand was read off by the town clerk. Quillow had folded his arms and crossed his legs and shut his eyes. He was thinking, but he looked like a sleeping toy.

"I, Hunder," droned the town clerk, "must have an apple pie each morning made of a thousand apples."

The baker jumped from his chair. "Why, that would use up all the apples and flour and shortening in town in a week and a fortnight," he cried. "And it would take me night and day to

46

make such a pie, so that I could bake no more pies or cakes or cookies, or blueberry muffins or cinnamon buns or cherry boats or strawberry tarts or plum puddings for the people of the town."

All of the councilmen moaned sadly because they loved the list of good things the baker had recited. Quillow still sat with his eyes closed.

"I, Hunder," went on the town clerk, "must have a house to live in by the time a week and a fortnight have passed."

The carpenter wept openly. "Why, I would have to work night and day to build a house for so large a giant in a week and a fortnight," sobbed the carpenter. "All my nephews and uncles and cousins would have to help me, and it would use up all the wood and pegs and hinges and glass in my shop and in the countryside."

The locksmith stood up and shook his fist in the direction of the hillside on which the giant lay snoring. "I will have to work night and day to make a brass key large enough to fit the keyhole in the front door of the house of so large a giant," he said. "It will use up all the brass in my shop and in the community."

"And I will have to make a candle for his bedside so large it will use up all the wick and tallow in my shop and the world," said the candlemaker.

"This is the final item," said the town clerk. "I, Hunder, must be told a tale each day to keep me amused."

Quillow opened his eyes and raised his hand. "*I* will be the teller of tales," he said. "*I* will keep the giant amused."

The town clerk put away his scroll.

"Does anyone have any idea of how to destroy the giant Hunder?" asked the candymaker.

"I could creep up on him in the dark and set fire to him with my lighter," said the lamplighter.

Quillow looked at him. "The fire of your lighter would not

harm him any more than a spark struck by a colt's shoe in a meadow," said Quillow.

"Quillow is right," said the blacksmith. "But I could build secretly at night an enormous catapult which would cast a gigantic stone and crush Hunder."

Quillow shook his head. "He would catch the stone as a child catches a ball," said Quillow, "and he would cast it back at the town and squash all our houses."

"I could put needles in his suit," said the tailor.

"I could put nails in his boots," said the cobbler.

"I could put oil in his chocolates," said the candymaker.

"I could put stones in his mutton," said the butcher.

"I could put tacks in his pies," said the baker.

"I could put gunpowder in his candles," said the candle-maker.

"I could make the handle of his brass key as sharp as a sword," said the locksmith.

"I could build the roof of his house insecurely so that it would fall on him," said the carpenter.

"The plans you suggest," said Quillow, "would merely annoy Hunder as the gadfly annoys the horse and the flea annoys the dog."

"Perhaps the Great Quillow has a plan of his own," said the blacksmith with a scornful laugh.

"Has the Great Quillow a plan?" asked the candymaker, with a faint sneer.

The little toymaker did not answer. The councillors got up and filed slowly and sadly from the council room. That night none of them wound the imaginary key in Quillow's back.

Quillow did not leave the council chamber for a long time, and when he walked through New Moon Street, all the shops of the councilmen were brightly lighted and noisily busy. There was a great ringing and scraping and thumping and rustling. The blacksmith was helping the locksmith make the great brass key for Hunder's house. The carpenter was sawing and planing enormous boards. The baker was shaping the crust for a gigantic pie, and his wife and apprentice were peeling a thousand apples. The butcher was dressing the first of the three sheep. The tailor was cutting the cloth for Hunder's jerkin. The cobbler was fitting together mammoth pieces of leather for Hunder's boots. The candymaker was piling all his chocolate upon his largest table, while his wife and daughter made soft filling in great kettles. The candlemaker had begun to build the monumental candle for Hunder's bedside.

As Quillow reached the door of his shop, the town clock in its steeple began to strike, the moon broke out of a patch of cloud and the toymaker stood with his hand on the door latch to watch the twelve little men in scarlet hats and jackets and pantaloons emerge, each from his own numeral, to make the night melodious with the sound of their silver hammers on the silver bells of the round white dial.

Inside his shop, Quillow lighted the green-shaded lamp over his workbench, which was littered with odds and ends and beginnings and middles of all kinds of toys. Working swiftly with his shining tools, Quillow began to make a figure eight inches high out of wire and cloth and leather and wood. When it was finished it looked like a creature you might come upon hiding behind a tulip or playing with toads. It had round eyes, a round nose, a wide mouth, and no hair. It was blue from head to foot. Its face was blue, its jacket was blue, its pantaloons were blue, and its feet were blue.

As Quillow stood examining the toy, the lamplighter stuck his head in the door without knocking, stared for a moment, and went away. Quillow smiled with satisfaction and began to make another blue man. By the time the first cock crowed he had made

49

ten blue men and put them away in a long wooden chest with a heavy iron clasp.

The lamplighter turned out the last street light, the sun rose, the crickets stopped calling and the clock struck five. Disturbed by the changing pattern of light and sound, the giant on the hillside turned in his sleep. Around a corner into New Moon Street tiptoed the town crier. "Sh!" he said to the lamplighter. "Don't wake the giant."

"Sh!" said the lamplighter. "His food may not be ready."

The town crier stood in the cobbled street and called softly, "Five o'clock, and all's well!"

All the doors in New Moon Street except Quillow's flew open.

"The pie is baked," said the baker.

"The chocolate is made," said the candymaker.

"The sheep are dressed," said the butcher.

"I worked all night on the great brass key," said the locksmith, "and the blacksmith helped me with his hammer and anvil."

"I have scarcely begun the enormous candle," said the candlemaker.

"I am weary of sawing and planing," said the carpenter.

"My fingers are already stiff," said the tailor, "and I have only just started the giant's jerkin."

"My eyes are tired," said the cobbler, "and I have hardly begun to make his boots."

The sun shone full on the giant's face, and he woke up and yawned loudly. The councillors jumped, and a hundred children hid in a hundred closets.

"Ho!" roared Hunder. It was the sign the blacksmith had waited for. He drove his wagon drawn by four horses into New Moon Street and climbed down.

"Ho!" roared the giant.

"Heave," grunted the councillors as they lifted the sheep onto

50

the wagon.

"Ho!" roared the giant.

"Heave," grunted the councillors, and they set the great chocolate in place.

Hunder watched the loading of the wagon, licking his lips and growling like a cave full of bulldogs.

The councillors climbed up on the wagon and the blacksmith yelled "Giddap!", and then "Whoa!" He glared about him. "Where is Quillow?" he demanded. "Where is that foolish little fellow?"

"He was in his shop at midnight," said the lamplighter, "making toys."

The nine other councillors snorted.

"He could have helped with the key," said the locksmith.

"The pie," said the baker.

"The sheep," said the butcher.

"The boots," said the cobbler.

At this, Quillow bounced out of his shop like a bird from a clock, bowing and smiling.

"Well!" snarled the blacksmith.

"Ho!" roared Hunder.

"Good morning," said Quillow. He climbed up on the wagon and the blacksmith spoke to each horse in turn. (Their names were Lobo, Bolo, Olob, and Obol.)

"I worked all night with my hammer and anvil," said the blacksmith as the horses lurched ahead, "helping the locksmith with the great brass key." He scowled at Quillow. "The lamplighter tells us *you* spent the night making toys."

"Making toys," said Quillow cheerily, "and thinking up a tale to amuse the giant Hunder."

The blacksmith snorted. "And a hard night you must have spent, hammering out your tale."

"And twisting it," said the locksmith.

51

"And levelling it," said the carpenter.

"And rolling it out," said the baker.

"And stitching it up," said the tailor.

"And fitting it together," said the cobbler.

"And building it around a central thread," said the candle-maker.

"And dressing it up," said the butcher.

"And making it not too bitter and not too sweet," said the candymaker.

When the wagon came to a stop at Hunder's feet, the giant clapped his hands, and Quillow and the councillors were blown to the ground. Hunder roared with laughter and unloaded the wagon in half a trice.

"Tell me your silly names," said Hunder, "and what you do." The new slaves of Hunder, all except Quillow, bowed in turn and told the giant who they were and what they did. Quillow remained silent.

"You, smallest of men, you with the white hair, who are *you*?" demanded Hunder.

"I am Quillow, the teller of tales," said the toymaker, but unlike the others, he did not bow to the giant.

"Bow," roared Hunder.

"Wow!" shouted Quillow.

The councillors started back in dismay at the toymaker's impertinence, their widening eyes on Hunder's mighty hands, which closed and then slowly opened. The black scowl cleared from the giant's brow and he laughed suddenly.

"You are a fairly droll fellow," he said. "Perhaps your tales will amuse me. If they do not, I will put you in the palm of my hand and blow you so far it will take men five days to find you. Now be off to your work, the rest of you!"

As the wagon carried the frightened councillors back to town, Quillow sat on the ground and watched the giant eat a sheep as

52

an ordinary man might eat a lark. "Now," said Hunder, "tell me a tale."

"Once upon a time," began Quillow, crossing his legs and tickling a cricket with a blade of grass, "a giant came to our town from a thousand leagues away, stepping over the hills and rivers. He was so mighty a giant that he could stamp upon the ground with his foot and cause the cows in the fields to turn flip-flops in the air and land on their feet again."

"Gauf!" growled Hunder, "I can stamp upon the ground with my foot and empty a lake of its water."

"I have no doubt of that, O Hunder," said Quillow, "for the thunder is your plaything and the mountains are your stool. But the giant who came over the hills and rivers many and many a year ago was a lesser giant than Hunder. He was weak. He fell ill of a curious malady. He was forced to run to the ocean and bathe in the yellow waters, for only the yellow waters in the middle of the sea could cure the giant."

"Rowf," snarled Hunder, picking up another sheep. "That giant was a goose, that giant was a grasshopper. Hunder is *never* sick." The giant smote his chest and then his stomach mighty blows without flinching, to show how strong he was.

"This other giant," said Quillow, "had no ailment of the chest or the stomach or the mouth or the ears or the eyes or the arms or the legs."

"Where else can a giant have an ailment?" demanded Hunder.

Quillow looked dreamily across the green valley towards the town, which was bright in the sun. "In the mind," said Quillow, "for the mind is a strange and intricate thing. In lesser men than Hunder, it is subject to mysterious maladies."

"Wumf," said the giant, beginning his third sheep. "Hunder's mind is strong like the rock." He smote himself heavily across the forehead without wincing.

53

"No one to this day knows what brought on this dreadful disease in the mind of the other giant," said Quillow. "Perhaps he killed a turtle after sundown, or ran clockwise thrice around a church in the dark of the moon, or slept too close to a field of asphodel."

Hunder picked up the pie and began to devour it. "Did this goose, this grasshopper, have pains in his head?" he asked. "Look, teller of tales!" Hunder banged his head savagely against a tree, and the trunk of the tree snapped in two. The giant grinned, showing his jagged teeth.

"This other giant," said Quillow, "suffered no pain. His symptoms were marvellous and dismaying. First he heard the word. For fifteen minutes one morning, beginning at a quarter of six he heard the word."

"Harumph!" said Hunder, finishing his pie and reaching for his chocolate. "What was the word the giant heard for fifteen minutes one day?"

"The word was 'woddly,'" said Quillow. "All words were one word to him. All words were 'woddly.'"

"All words are different to Hunder," said the giant. "And do you call this a tale you have told me? A blithering goose of a giant heard a word and you call that a tale to amuse Hunder?"

Quillow arose as the clock in the steeple struck six and the scarlet figures came out to play the silver bells.

"I hear all words," said Hunder. "This is a good chocolate; otherwise I should put you in the palm of my hand and blow you over the housetops."

"I shall bring you a better tale tomorrow," said Quillow. "Meanwhile, be sure to see the first star over your left shoulder, do not drink facing downstream, and always sleep with your heart to the east."

"Why should Hunder practise this foolish rigmarole?" asked the giant.

"No one knows to this day," said Quillow, "what caused the weird things in the mind of the other giant." But Hunder gave only a murmurous growl in reply, for he had lain down again on the hillside and closed his eyes. Quillow smiled as he saw that the giant lay with his heart to the east.

The toymaker spent the day making twenty more little blue men and when the first owl hooted he stood in the doorway of his shop and whistled. The hundred children collected in the cobbled street before the toyshop from every nook and corner and cranny and niche of the town. "Go to your homes," said Quillow, "each Sue and John of you, each Nora and Joe, and tell your fathers and mothers to come to the merry-go-round in the carnival grounds one quarter-hour before the moon comes over the hill. Say that Quillow has a plan to destroy the giant Hunder."

The group of children broke like the opening of a rose and the cobbled streets rang with the sound of their running.

Even the scowling blacksmith, the scornful lamplighter, the mumbling town crier, and the fussy town clerk (who had spent the day searching for an ancient treaty the people of the town had once signed with a giant) came at the appointed hour to hear what Quillow had to say.

"What is this clown's whim that brings us here like sheep?" demanded the blacksmith.

Quillow climbed up on the merry-go-round, sat on a swan, and spoke. At first there was a restless stir like wind in the grass, but as Quillow explained his plan, even the chattering wives fell silent. Quillow finished speaking as the moon peeped over the hill, and the hundred men and the hundred women and the hundred children straggled away from the carnival grounds.

"It will never work," said the lamplighter.

"It is worth trying," said the candymaker.

"I have a better plan," said the town crier. "Let all the women and all the children stand in the streets and gaze sorrowfully at the giant, and perhaps he will go away."

His wife took him by the arm and led him home. "We will try Quillow's plan," she said. "He has a magic, the little man."

The next morning, just as the clock in the steeple struck five the weary blacksmith, with Quillow sitting beside him, drove the wagon loaded with three sheep and a fresh apple pie and another monster chocolate to where the giant sat on the hillside. Hunder unloaded the wagon in a third of a trice, placed the food beside him on the hill, and began to gnaw at a sheep. "Tell me a tale, smallest of men," he said, "and see to it that I do not nod or I shall put you in the palm of my hand and blow you through yonder cloud."

"Once upon a time," began Quillow, "there was a king named Anderblusdaferafan, and he had three sons named Ufrebrodoborobe, Quamdelrodolanderay, and Tristolcomo-farasee."

"Those names are hard names," said Hunder. "Tell me those names again that I may remember them." So Quillow started over slowly with "Once upon a time," and again the giant made him repeat the names.

"Why did this king and his sons have such long and difficult names?" demanded Hunder, eating his second sheep.

"Ah," said Quillow, "it was because of the king's mother, whose name was Isoldasadelofandaloo."

"Tell me her name once more," said Hunder, "that I may remember it." So Quillow told him the name again slowly.

Thus the wily Quillow, who really had thought of no tale to tell, wasted the long minutes as the hands of the clock in the steeple crept around the dial. As they neared a quarter of six o'clock, Quillow went on. "One day as the king and his sons were riding through the magical forest," he said, "they came upon a woddly. Woddly woddly woddly. Woddly woddly

56

woddly."

The giant's eyes grew narrow, then wide.

"Woddly woddly woddly," said Quillow, "woddly woddly woddly." The giant dropped the chocolate he was eating. "Say it with words!" he bellowed. "You say naught but 'woddly'."

Quillow looked surprised. "Woddly woddly woddly woddly woddly, woddly, woddly woddly woddly," he said. "Woddly woddly woddly."

"Can this be the malady come upon me?" cried the giant. He caught the toymaker up in his hand. "Or do you seek to frighten Hunder?" he roared.

"Woddly woddly woddly," said Quillow, trembling in spite of himself, as he pointed to a farmer in a field and to a child gathering cowslips and to the town crier making his rounds. "Woddly woddly woddly," repeated Quillow.

The giant dropped Quillow and arose. He strode to where the farmer stood and picked him up. "Say words!" bawled Hunder. "Say many words!"

"Woddly," said the farmer, and Hunder dropped him in the field and turned to the child.

"What is your name?" roared Hunder.

"Woddly woddly," said the child.

Hunder stepped over to the town crier. "What is the time of day?" he bellowed.

"Woddly woddly," said the town crier.

Then Hunder shouted questions at men and women and children who came running into the streets. He asked them how old they were, and what day it was, and where they were going, and how they were feeling. And they said "Woddly" and "Woddly woddly" and "Woddly woddly woddly."

Hunder strode back across the green valley to where Quillow sat brushing flies off the half-eaten chocolate. "It is the malady! I have heard the word! It is the malady!" cried Hunder. "What

57

am I to do to cure the malady?"

Just then the clock in the steeple struck six, and as the scarlet men came out to play the bells, Quillow spoke reproachfully. "I was telling you how the king and his three sons rode through the magical forest," he said, "when you picked me up and flung me to the earth and ran away, leaving your chocolate uneaten."

The giant sat on the ground, panting heavily, his lower teeth showing. "I heard the word," he said. "All men said the word."

"What word," asked Quillow

"Woddly," said the giant.

"That is but the first symptom," said Quillow reassuringly, "and it has passed. Look at the chimneys of the town. Are they not red?"

Hunder looked. "Yes, the chimneys are red," said Hunder. "Why do you ask if the chimneys are red?"

"So long as the chimneys are red," said Quillow, "you have no need to worry, for when the second symptom is felt, all the chimneys of the town turn black."

"I see only red chimneys," said the giant. "But what could have caused Hunder to hear the word?" he asked as he hurled the half eaten chocolate far away over the roofs of the town.

"Perhaps," said Quillow, "you stepped on a centaur's grave, waked the sleeping unicorn or whistled on Saint Nillin's Day."

Hunder the giant rested badly on the hillside that night, twisting and turning in his sleep, tormented by ominous dreams. While he slept, the youngest and most agile men of the town, in black smocks and slippered feet, climbed to the roofs of the houses and shops, each carrying a full pail and a brush, and painted all the chimneys black.

Quillow, the toymaker, worked busily all night, and by the dark hour before the dawn, had made twenty more blue men so that he now had fifty blue men in all. He put the new ones with the others he had made, in the large chest with the iron clasp.

58

As the first birds twittered in the trees, the lamplighter and the town crier came into the toyshop. Quillow was repairing a doll for a little girl who was ill. He smiled and bowed to his friends confidently, but the palms of their hands were moist and the roofs of their mouths were dry.

"Perhaps he will detect your trick," said the lamplighter.

"Perhaps he will smash all our houses," said the town crier.

As the three men talked, they heard the giant stirring on the hillside. He rubbed his eyes with his great knuckles, yawned with the sound of a sinking ship, and stretched his powerful arms. The toymaker and the lamplighter and the town crier watched through a window and held their breath.

Hunder sat up, staring at the ground and running his fingers through his hair. Then slowly he lifted his head and looked at the town. He closed his eyes tightly and opened them again and stared. His mouth dropped open and he lurched to his feet. "The chimneys!" he bellowed. "The chimneys are black! The malady is upon me again!"

Quillow began to scamper through the cobbled streets and across the green valley as the giant's eyes rolled and his knees trembled. "Teller of tales, smallest of men!" bellowed Hunder. "Tell me what I must do. The chimneys are black!" Quillow reached the feet of the giant, panting and flushed. "Look, teller of tales," said the giant, "name me fairly the colour of yonder chimneys."

Quillow turned and looked toward the town. "The chimneys are red, O Hunder," he said. "The chimneys are red. See how they outdo the red rays of the sun."

"The rays of the sun are red," said Hunder, "but the chimneys of the town are black."

"You tremble," said Quillow, "and your tongue hangs out, and these are indeed the signs of the second symptom. But still there is no real danger, for you do not see the blue men. Or *do*

59

you see the blue men, O Hunder?" he asked.

"I see the men of the town standing in the streets and staring at me," said Hunder. "But their faces are white and they wear clothes of many colours. Why do you ask me if I see blue men?"

Quillow put on a look of grave concern. "When you see the blue men," he said, "it is the third and last symptom of the malady. If that should happen, you must rush to the sea and bathe in the yellow waters or your strength will become the strength of a kitten." The giant groaned. "Perhaps if you fast for a day and a night," said Quillow, "the peril will pass."

"I will do as you say, teller of tales," said the giant, "for you are wise beyond the manner of men. Bring me no food today, tell me no tale." And with a moan Hunder sat back upon the hillside and covered his eyes with his hands.

When Quillow returned to the town, the people cheered him softly and the children flung flowers at his feet. But the blacksmith was sceptical. "The giant is still there on the hillside," he said. "I shall save my cheers and my flowers until the day he is gone, if that day shall ever come." And he stalked back to his smithy to help the locksmith make the great brass key for Hunder's front door.

That noon there was enough mutton and pie and chocolate for all the people of the town, and they ate merrily and well.

Hunder the giant fretted and worried so profoundly during the day that he fell quickly to sleep as the night came. It was a night without moon or stars, as Quillow had hoped. A town owl who lived on the roof of the tavern—at the Sign of the Clock and Soldier—was surprised at the soft and shadowy activities of the toymaker. The bat and the firefly hovered about him in wonder as he worked secretly and swiftly in the green valley at the feet of the snoring giant. The squirrel and the nightingale watched like figures in a tapestry as he dug and planted in the woods at the giant's head. If the giant thrashed suddenly in his sleep or

60

groaned, the cricket and the frog fell silent in high anxiety. When Quillow's work was finished and he returned to his shop, the bat and the firefly moved in dreamy circles, the squirrel and the nightingale stirred freely again, and the cricket and the frog began to sing. The owl on the roof of the Clock and Soldier nodded and slept. Quillow lay down on his workbench and closed his eyes.

When the scarlet men played the bells of five o'clock, and the first birds twittered in the trees and the grey light came, Quillow awoke and opened his door. The town crier stood in the cobbled street in front of the shop. "Cry the hour," said Quillow. "Cry all's well."

"Five o'clock!" cried the town crier. "Five o'clock and all's well!"

The people crept out of their houses and on the hillside across the green valley, Hunder the giant stirred and yawned and stretched and rubbed his eyes and sat up. He saw that the chimneys were still black, but he grinned at them and winked. "The malady passes," said Hunder. "I see men with white faces wearing clothes of many colours, but I see no blue men." He flexed the muscles of his powerful arms and he smote himself mighty blows upon his brow and chest and stomach. "Ho, councillors!" roared Hunder, "bring me my sheep and pie and my chocolate, for I have a vast hunger."

The people fled from the streets, and behind the barred doors and shuttered windows of their houses they listened and trembled. The baker, the butcher, and the candymaker hid under their beds. They had prepared no meal for the giant and they were afraid for their lives. But the brave little toymaker, his white hair flowing like the dandelion clock in the morning wind, ran through the cobbled streets and across the green valley and stood at the giant's feet.

"Behold, I am still a whole man!" bellowed the giant,

61

thumping his brow. "I have heard the word and I have seen the black chimneys, but I have not beheld the blue men."

"That is well," said Quillow, "for he who beholds the blue men must bathe in the yellow waters in the middle of the sea, or else he will dwindle, first to the height of the pussy willow, then to the height of the daffodil, then to the height of the violet, until finally he becomes a small voice in the grass, lost in the thundering of the crickets."

"But *I* shall remain stronger than the rock and taller than the oak," said Hunder, and he clapped his hands together.

"If you are stronger than the rock and taller than the oak," said Quillow, "then stamp on the ground and make yonder cow in the field turn a flip-flop."

Hunder stood up and chortled with glee. "Behold, smallest of men," he said, "I will make the cow turn twice in the air." He brought his right foot down upon the earth sharply and heavily. The cow turned a double flip-flop in the field, Quillow bounced as high as the giant's belt, and great boughs fell from trees. But the giant had no eyes for these familiar wonders. He stared at something new under the sun, new and small and terrible. The blue men had come. The blue men were popping high into the air. They popped up in the valley and they popped up in the woods. They popped up from behind stones and they popped up from behind cowslips. They popped up in front of Hunder and they popped up behind him and under him and all around him.

"The blue men!" cried Hunder. "The blue men have come! The world is filled with little blue men!"

"I see no blue men," said Quillow, "but you have begun to shrink like the brook in dry weather, and that is the sign of the third symptom."

"The sea! The sea! Point me to the sea!" bellowed Hunder, who now stood shivering and shaking.

"It is many leagues to the east," said Quillow. "Run quickly towards the rising sun and bathe in the yellow waters in the middle of the sea."

Hunder the giant ran toward the rising sun, and the town trembled as he ran. Pictures fell from walls and plates from plate rails and bricks from chimneys. The birds flew and the rabbits scampered. The cows turned flip-flops in the fields and the brook jumped out of its bed.

A fortnight later a traveller from afar, stopping at the Sign of the Clock and Soldier, told the innkeeper a marvellous tale of how a giant, panting and moaning like a forest fire, had stumbled down out of the mountains and plunged into the sea, flailing and threshing, and babbling of yellow waters and black chimneys and little blue men; and of how he had floundered farther and farther out to sea until at last he sank beneath the waves, starting a mighty tide rolling to the shore and sending up water spouts as high as the heavens. Then the giant was seen no more, and the troubled waters quieted as the sea resumed its inscrutable cycle of tides under the sun and the moon.

The innkeeper told this tale to the blacksmith, and the blacksmith told it to the locksmith, and the locksmith told it to the baker, and the baker told it to the butcher, and the butcher told it to the tailor, and the tailor told it to the cobbler, and the cobbler told it to the candymaker, and the candymaker told it to the candlemaker, and the candlemaker told it to the town crier, and the town crier told it to the lamplighter, and the lamplighter told it to the toymaker.

As the lamplighter spoke, Quillow put the finishing touches on a new toy whistling softly, his eyes sparkling. The lamplighter saw that the toy was a tiny replica of Quillow himself.

"What do you do with that?" he asked.

"You put it in the palm of your hand, like this," said Quillow, and he put the figure in the palm of his hand. "And then you blow like this." He blew, and the miniature Quillow floated slowly through the air and drifted gently to the floor. "I think it will amuse the children," said the little toymaker. "I got the idea from the giant."

The Ogre Courting

By Juliana Horatia Ewing

The local Ogre was so impressed by the thrifty qualities of a poor farmer's daughter that he was determined she must become his twenty-fifth bride. His demands for a dowry were refused and reluctantly he had to accept the conditions laid down by Molly before she would agree to the marriage ...

In days when ogres were still the terror of certain districts, there was one who had long kept a whole neighbourhood in fear without anyone daring to dispute his tyranny.

By thefts and exactions, by heavy ransoms from merchants too old and tough to be eaten, in one way and another, the Ogre had become very rich; and although those who knew could tell of huge cellars full of gold and jewels, and yards and barns groaning with the weight of stolen goods, the richer he grew the more anxious and covetous he became. Moreover, day by day, he added to his stores; for though (like most ogres) he was as stupid as he was strong, no one had ever been found, by force or fraud, to get the better of him.

What he took from the people was not their heaviest grievance. Even to be killed and eaten by him was not the chance they thought of most. A man can die but once; and if he is a sailor, a shark may eat him, which is not so much better than being devoured by an ogre. No, that was not the worst. The worst was this—he would keep getting married! And, as he liked little wives, all the short little women lived in fear and dread. And as his wives always died very soon, he was constantly courting fresh ones.

Some said he ate his wives; some said he tormented them, and others said he only worked them to death. Everybody knew it was not a desirable match, and yet there was not a father who dared refuse his daughter if she were asked for. The Ogre only cared for two things in a woman—he liked her to be little, and a good housewife.

Now it was when the Ogre had just lost his twenty-fourth wife (within the memory of man) that these two qualities were eminently united in the person of the smallest and most notable woman of the district—the daughter of a certain poor farmer. He was so poor that he could not afford properly to furnish a dowry for his daughter, who had in consequence remained single beyond her first youth. Everybody felt sure that Managing Molly must now be married to the Ogre. The tall girls stretched themselves till they looked like maypoles and said: "Poor thing!" The slatterns gossiped from house to house, the heels of their shoes clacking as they went, and cried that this was what came of being too thrifty.

And sure enough, in due time, the giant widower came to the farmer as he was in the field looking over his crops, and proposed for Molly there and then. The farmer was so much put out that he did not know what he said in reply, either when he was saying it, or afterwards, when his friends asked about it. But he did remember that the Ogre had invited himself to sup at the farm that day week.

Managing Molly did not distress herself at the news.

"Do what I bid you, and say as I say," said she to her father; "and if the Ogre does not change his mind, at any rate you shall not come empty-handed out of the business."

66

By his daughter's desire the farmer now procured a large number of hares, and a barrel of white wine, which expenses completely emptied his slender hoard. Molly herself went around to all her neighbours, and borrowed a lot of new household linen, with which she filled the kitchen shelves. On the day of the Ogre's visit, she made a delicious and savoury stew with the hares in the biggest pickling tub, and the wine-barrel was set on a bench near the table.

When the Ogre came, Molly served up the stew, and the Ogre sat down to sup, his head just touching the kitchen rafters. The stew was perfect, and there was plenty of it. For what Molly and her father ate was hardly to be counted in the tub-full. The Ogre was very much pleased, and said politely:

"I'm afraid, my dear, that you have been put to great trouble and expense on my account. I have a large appetite, and like to sup well."

"Don't mention it, sir," said Molly. "The fewer rats the more corn. How do *you* cook them?"

"Not one of all the extravagant hussies I have had as wives ever cooked them at all," said the Ogre; and he thought to himself: "Such a stew, and of rats! What frugality! What a housewife!" "I suppose you spin?" he inquired.

Molly held out her hand, in which was a linen towel made from the last month's spinning, and said: "All that came off my wheel last month."

But as her hand was raised towards the shelves, the Ogre thought that all the linen he saw there was from thread of her spinning; and his admiration grew every moment.

When he tasted the wine, he was no less pleased, for it was of the best.

"This, at any rate, must have cost you a great deal, neighbour," said the Ogre, drinking the farmer's health as Molly left the room.

"I don't know that rotten apples could be better used," said the farmer; "But I leave all that to Molly. Do you brew at home?"

"We give *our* rotten apples to the pigs," growled the Ogre. "But things will be better ordered when she is my wife."

The Ogre was now in great haste to conclude the match, and asked what dowry the farmer would give his daughter.

"I should never dream of giving a dowry with Molly," said the farmer boldly. "Whoever gets her gets dowry enough. On the contrary, I shall expect a good round sum from the man who deprives me of her. Our wealthiest farmer is just widowed, and therefore sure to be in a hurry for marriage. He has an eye to the main chance, and would not grudge to pay well for such a wife, I'll warrant."

"I'm no churl myself," said the Ogre, who was anxious to secure this thrifty bride at any price; and he named a large sum of money, thinking: "We shall live on rats henceforward, and the money saved on beef and mutton will soon cover the dowry."

"Double that, and we'll see," said the farmer stoutly.

But the Ogre became angry, and cried:

"What are you thinking of, man? Who is to hinder my carrying your lass off, without 'with your leave' or 'by your leave', dowry or none?"

"How little you know her!" said the farmer. "She is so firm that she would be cut to pieces sooner than give you any benefit of her thrift, unless you dealt fairly in the matter."

"Well, well," said the Ogre, "let us meet each other." And he named a sum larger than he at first proposed, and less than the farmer had asked. This the farmer agreed to, as it was enough to make him prosperous for life.

"Bring it in a sack tomorrow morning," said he to the Ogre, "and then you can speak to Molly; she's gone to bed now."

The next morning accordingly, the Ogre appeared, carrying

the dowry in a sack, and Molly came to meet him.

"There are two things," said she, "I would ask of any lover of mine: a new farmhouse, built as I should direct, with a view to economy; and a featherbed of fresh goose feathers, filled when the old woman plucks her geese. If I don't sleep well, I cannot work well."

"That is better than asking for finery," thought the Ogre; "and after all, the house will be my own." So to save the expense of labour he built it himself, and worked hard, day after day, under Molly's orders, till winter came. Then it was finished.

"Now for the feather-bed," said Molly. "I'll make the ticking, and when the old woman plucks her geese, I'll let you know."

When it snows, they say the old woman up yonder is plucking geese; so at the first snowstorm Molly sent for the Ogre.

"Now you see the feathers falling," said she, "so fill up the bed."

"How am I to catch them?" cried the Ogre.

"Stupid! don't you see them lying there in a heap?" cried Molly. "Get a shovel, and set to work."

The Ogre accordingly carried in shovelfuls of snow to the bed, but as it melted as fast as he put it in, his labour never seemed done. Towards night the room got so cold that the snow would not melt, and now the bed was soon filled.

Molly hastily covered it with sheets and blankets, and said:

"Pray rest here tonight, and tell me if the bed is not comfort itself. Tomorrow we will be married."

So the tired Ogre lay down on the bed he had filled, but do what he could, he could not get warm.

"The sheets must be damp," said he, and in the morning he woke with such horrible pains in his bones that he could hardly move, and half the bed had melted away. "It's no use," he groaned, "she's a very managing woman, but to sleep on such a bed would be the death of me." And he went off home as quickly

69

as he could, before Managing Molly could call upon him to be married; for she was so managing, that he was more than half afraid of her already.

When Molly found that he had gone, she sent the farmer after him.

"What does he want?" cried the Ogre, when they told him the farmer was at the door.

"He says the bride is waiting for you," was the reply.

"Tell him I'm too ill to be married," said the Ogre.

But the messenger soon returned:

"He says she wants to know what you will give her to make up for the disappointment."

"She's got the dowry, and the farm, and the feather-bed," groaned the Ogre; "what more is there she can possibly want?"

But again the messenger returned:

"She says you've pressed the feather-bed flat, and she wants some more goose feathers."

"There are geese enough in the yard!" yelled the Ogre. "Let him drive them home, and if he has another word to say, to put him down to roast."

The farmer, who overheard this order, lost no time in taking his leave, and as he passed through the yard he drove home as fine a flock of geese as you will see on a common.

It is said that the Ogre never recovered from the effects of sleeping on the old woman's feathers, and was less powerful than before.

As for Managing Molly, being now well dowered, she had no lack of offers of marriage, and was soon mated to her complete satisfaction.

The Wicked Giant of Stone

A South American Story

Retold by John Meehan

It seemed impossible to harm the giant Sinulu, as he was made of stone. When eventually all the men had been killed off it was left to a woman and a humming-bird to free the country of a terrible tyrant.

In far-off days, there lived in the land now belonging to the Onas a giant called Sinulu. He had been carved out of rock by the God of the Glaciers, and nothing could harm his body as it was made of stone. His eyes were human and his feet were flesh, but this was a secret that few had heard.

Sinulu lived alone, for none who knew of him dared cross the narrow neck of land that joined his dominions to the mainland. By day he roamed the countryside and the earth shuddered at the approach of his pounding footsteps while the mountains felt like ant-hills as he towered above them.

Sinulu was never without his terrible whip with its twelve whistling thongs. Often, for sport, he would crack it against the forests and bellow with laughter as the trees bent like matchsticks before it. The crack and the swish of the terrible whip could be heard leagues away on the mainland, and the people there crouched in terror as the twelve savage thongs whistled through the air and turned the winds into hurricanes.

One day a wandering tribe of huntsmen and their wives, who knew nothing of the giant, crossed the causeway from the mainland and entered Sinulu's dominions. They were hunters of guanaco, the wild llama with red-brown fleece that lived in those parts. Within an hour of their arrival the hunters were seen by Sinulu.

The giant became so furious that he began to dance with rage. Faster and faster he danced until the ground heaved and rolled, mountains cracked apart, the seas swelled and the wind roared itself hoarse. The strip of land between the mainland and Sinulu's domain shivered and split and shattered to a million pieces that slipped into the frothing ocean. There was no way back for the wandering huntsmen.

When he saw this, the giant became calmer and the earth settled and was still. In four huge strides he moved down from his home in the mountains on to the plain, where the terrified hunters huddled together.

"Now I have you!" he stormed. "Now you are mine! There is no escape. I shall teach you such a lesson for daring to come here unasked. You will never forget it." At this he laughed so fiercely that the poor huntsmen were blown flat on the ground.

Sinulu made them his slaves. He sent them hunting day and night for guanaco, he forced them to fell trees till their strength was gone, or cut huge steps in the mountains so that he could move about more easily. Worst of all, he even set them to fight and kill each other for his amusement. Any man who disobeyed was treated to a taste of the cruel whip with the twelve whistling thongs after which he quickly learned obedience. He gave them no shelter, and kept them so busy at his tasks that they had neither time nor energy to build their own huts. They had to bake him two hundred loaves a day and make him a hundred

72

cheeses of goats' milk. Yet such was his appetite that he ate all their food as well.

The men grew so weak that many of them could no longer work, but he lashed them with his whistling, twelve-thonged whip and said that not a handful of food would they have unless it was earned by a good day's labour. And so, worn out by cruel punishments, lack of food and exhausting effort, the men began to die. And as the men died, Sinulu replaced them with the women of the tribe. In time all the men died and he forced the women to hunt and dig and carry loads and even fight among themselves for his amusement as the men had. He had no pity, for his heart was stone like his body. The eye of the sun had never seen a harsher tyrant.

One afternoon a woman of the tribe sat weeping bitterly when a humming-bird came up to her. The bird's wings whirred about the woman and she looked up with the tears pouring from her eyes.

"My poor woman, why do you weep so bitterly?" asked the humming-bird, still flying in wide circles. "Your sorrow must be truly great. Tell me why you grieve so?"

"As you say, my sorrow is great," said the woman. "I have been sent here by Sinulu to fell him a tree and I can't even lift the axe. I'm so weak, so very weak." she began to cry again.

"I know about the wicked Sinulu," said the humming-bird. "My childhood friends were the gull and the duck, and they told me all about him and his cruelty."

At the mention of cruelty, the woman looked up once more.

"I know about it too," she said. "If I don't take back this tree, Sinulu will beat me with his terrible whip with twelve whistling thongs. And I can't fell the tree. I can't, I can't. I've no strength left."

"Dry your eyes, woman," said the humming-bird. "Have no more fears for I have come here to save you all."

The woman stopped crying when she heard this.

"You? Save us from Sinulu?" her eyes widened in disbelief. "If it wasn't so tragic I'd laugh," she said. "What can a tiny, feeble little bird like you do against Sinulu?"

The humming-bird whirred angrily at this description of himself.

"Strength isn't everything, my good woman," he said.

"That may be," said the woman. "But Sinulu has a body of stone. Nothing can hurt him. Arrows and knives are of no use against such as he. What can we do?"

"Strength isn't everything," repeated the humming-bird. "Courage and intelligence are just as important. And I shall save you from Sinulu because I'm more intelligent than he is. Listen to me while I tell you how."

The bird told the woman that although Sinulu had a body of stone, his feet were flesh and bone. What they must do was collect the sharpest and prickliest and biggest thorns they could find and set them on the earth so that the giant would walk on them.

"You do that and the rest will be easy," assured the humming-bird. "You leave it to me."

The women obeyed the bird's instructions. They collected the sharpest and prickliest and biggest thorns they could find and laid many hundreds of them upon the ground between themselves and the giant.

"Now you must sit down and rest," said the humming-bird. "Do not do any of the tasks that Sinulu has given you. Just sit here and wait. He'll get angry, you'll see. He'll get furious because you haven't felled the trees as he ordered. Then he'll come rushing down here and the thorns will stab into his feet."

The women sat down as the humming-bird had said and soon the air was filled with an enormous bellow of rage that made the mountains shiver.

75

"You lazy, good-for-nothing women," roared the giant. "What do you mean by lying about all day long?"

He came pounding down upon them, waving his terrible whip about his head, his feet shaking the plain so that it felt like a rolling sea.

"Why haven't you done what I told you?" he bellowed. "Where are the trees I ordered, and my cheeses and my loaves? Where AAARRRGHHHHH!"

Sinulu screamed with a violence that was like the sound of a thousand trumpets and clutched wildly at his left foot.

"Aaaarrrghhh! Aaaaarrrrrgghhhh!" he shrieked. He put his foot down and tried to run clear of the thorns, but they were everywhere around him, and with each step more stabbed into his great, fleshy feet, making them look like porcupines.

Sinulu sank heavily to the ground.

"Come here and pull these thorns out of my feet," he roared. "Quickly, quickly! Get them out. Hurry, women, HURRY!"

All the time, the humming-bird had been whirring about near the women, waiting for this moment.

"Go as the giant orders," he said. "Take out the thorns and drive in a knife instead. Go. All of you."

The women did as they were told. First they pulled out the thorns so that Sinulu sighed with relief. Then, in an instant, they had stabbed home two sharp-pointed knives, one in each of his feet, until they were embedded up to the hilt in his flesh.

"AAAAAAAAARRRRRRRRRGGGGGGGHHHHHHH!"

"Now bring two stakes quickly," said the humming-bird.

Two women rushed up with the pointed sticks and, directed by the humming-bird, plunged them into Sinulu's eyes and blinded him.

"Make a fire," ordered the humming-bird. "There's not a moment to lose. A fire, please! A huge one. Build it over the giant."

76

Logs and branches and dried leaves were heaped on the blinded giant who rolled and whimpered in agony. With every second his strength was ebbing away through the soles of his feet. As soon as he was covered, the wood was lit and in seconds became a raging bonfire.

"We are saved," yelled the women who began to dance joyfully round the fire. There was a violent explosion, flames and wood shot into the air and the giant's body burst into a thousand pieces. "We are saved! We are saved!" chanted the women.

"Not yet," warned the humming-bird. "You are not saved yet. Each piece of Sinulu's body can grow into another giant, just as terrible as before. You must burn every piece. Every single piece!"

Hastily the women did as they were told, and when the last of the thousand fragments was roasting on the fire, again shouted "We are saved! We are saved!"

"Not yet," said the humming-bird. "Good women, you are not saved yet. There still remains Sinulu's heart. Unless you burn it to ashes, it will grow into another giant, ten times as cruel as before. Burn it."

The women did not need a second bidding and soon Sinulu's heart was roasted to a cinder on the bonfire. Now, at last, the women were really free. They danced and shouted and sang, and the valley echoed to the sound of happy laughter for the first time in many years. But the woman who had been weeping by the roadside reminded them suddenly of the humming-bird. It was he who had saved them.

"You are our saviour," she told him. "We owe you our lives and our liberty. You must become our King."

The humming-bird would not accept the crown. He told the women that if they wished to reward him, then all he asked was that they should make him a beautiful garden and fill it with

77

sweet-smelling flowers which would be fountains for him to drink from.

And this they agreed to do.

David and Goliath

By Walter de la Mare

In traditional tales and folklore a giant represented an evil threat of some kind. This great force of evil was usually overcome, using superhuman strength or guile, by the force of good. Even the Bible has its own giant, as all those who know the story of David and Goliath will remember.

When again the Philistines gathered an army together for war, they marched into the territory of Judah, and pitched their camp above the Valley of Elah, and on the steeps of a mountain ridge west of Bethlehem. And the host of Israel lay on the northern height of the valley, so that the two armies were face to face, and in sight of one another; the Philistines occupying the mountain on the one side, and Saul and his army occupying the mountain on the other side, with the wide valley and ravine between them. Through this ravine a pebbly brook coursed down among its rocks from the mountains above.

Now in the ranks of the Philistines at this time was a giant of prodigious strength and girth and stature, whose name was Goliath. He was of the city of Gath, and his four sons who were as yet in their childhood there, grew up to be giants like him; and one of them had six fingers on either hand, and on either foot six toes. From the crown of his head to the sole of his foot Goliath stood six cubits and a span. And he was the champion of the army of the Philistines.

While the day of battle was still in the balance, and neither army moved, morning and evening this Goliath would issue out from among the tents of the camp of the Philistines, stride down into the valley and there, in full view of both armies, would roar out his challenge, defying all Israel. Unlike his fellows in the ranks who were dressed in kilts with a pleated head-cap strapped under the chin, and who, apart from spear and broad-sword, carried only a two-handled shield or wore a cuirass of leather, he was clad from head to foot in armour of brass. A helmet of bronze was upon his head; a bronze coat of mail loose and supple covered his body, the scales of it overlapping one above another like the scales of a fish; and it weighed five thousand shekels of brass. Greaves also of bronze covered his shins, and a javelin of bronze hung between his shoulders. The haft of the spear he carried was like the beam of a weaver's loom, and the pointed head of iron upon it weighed six hundred shekels. And there went out before him a crook-backed Philistine who in stature was a dwarf by comparison, and he carried the giant's shield.

Now when this champion had bawled his challenge, and no man made answer, he would begin to taunt and mock at the Israelites.

"Why, forsooth," he would shout against them, "have you come out in your rabble against the Philistines, and why have you set yourselves in battle array, seeing that the quarrel between us may be decided here and now? Here stand I, a warrior of the princes of Philistia; and there sit you, servants of Saul. If there be any man among you with the courage of a sheep, drive him down to meet me, face to face. For I swear by Dagon that if he prevail against me and kill me, then shall the Philistines become the slaves of Israel, to hew them wood and draw them water. But if, as I surely shall, I prevail against him, and fell him to the dust with this spear in my hand, then shall Israel be the slaves of the Philistines. Hai, now! Yet again this day I defy the armies of Israel. If man among you there is none to meet me, call on Jehovah to smite me with his thunderbolt! Peradventure he will answer!"

He clashed with his spear upon his breastplate, shouting derision. And the troops of Israel who heard him were dismayed. There were many men among them of tried valour and skill in battle, but not one ready to go out against this giant in single combat, with even a hope of triumphing over him. And defeat would bring disaster.

So morning and evening, Goliath would come striding down out of the camp of the Philistines, yell aloud his challenge, and pour out his taunts and insults. And the Philistines laughed to hear him.

Now of the eight sons of Jesse, who was himelf too old for the hardships of war, the three eldest, Eliab, Abindab and Shammah, were serving in the ranks of the army under Saul. But David, the youngest, was with his father in Bethlehem, keeping his sheep.

When one evening he returned home, his father bade him set out on the morrow for the camp of the army of Israel to see how his brothers fared.

"And take with thee," he said, "a bushel of this parched corn, and these ten loaves and these ten cheeses; and run to the camp and bring me news, for it is many days since we had word of them."

The parched or roasted corn and the flat round loaves were for David's brothers, and the curd cheeses were for a present to the captain in command of their thousand. For Saul and they themselves and all the men of Israel were above the valley of Elah, confronting the Philistines.

Next morning, then, as soon as the first flush of dawn appeared in the sky, David rose up and having left his sheep in charge of a herdsman, set out for the camp, a journey of twelve miles. He went rejoicing on his way. After the brief time he had spent in the service of the king, he had fretted at remaining at home with his father, keeping his sheep. He pined to be with his brothers, fighting for Israel.

When he came to the hills on which Saul's army was entrenched, the whole camp was astir. For army against army, Israel and the Philistines were ready and in array. He heard that battle might be joined that very morning. On fire with eagerness to see what was afoot, David gave all that he had brought with him into the hands of the keeper who had charge of the baggage, and ran off with all speed to seek out his brothers. Their quarters were in the forefront of the camp. There he found them and saluted them. "Peace be with you!" he said. And he gave them his father's message, and talked with them there.

And as he talked with them, his eyes ranged eagerly over the camp of the Philistines on the heights above and beyond the valley. Their bright-dyed tents in the crystal clear air shone in their colours in the sun. He could even count their chariots with their horses and charioteers. And the mountain-side was thick with men moving—like an ant-hill in midsummer, when its warriors prepare to sally out to attack a neighbouring tribe.

Curious and intent, he watched every movement, and at the same time questioned his brothers of what he saw, the numbers, the regiments, the commanders, the chances of the battle.

The day was yet early, and even as he watched, there showed a stir on the outskirts of the enemy's camp, and there issued out of it from among the host of the Philistines, smalled in the distance and alone but for his armour-bearer, the giant, Goliath.

With slow and ponderous tread he advanced down the slope into the valley until he was a little beyond midway between the two camps, and a rabble of his comrades followed after him, though afar off.

He came to a standstill, and brandishing his bronze-tipped

82

spear on high, he cried out as he had cried before, and roared out his challenge against Israel. The hoarse echoes of his voice rang among the hills; the sun beat down upon the burnished fish-scales of his armour, and gleamed upon his helmet. David could well-nigh see the glittering of his eyes in his great face.

At sight of him he had fallen silent. He stood stock-still like an image carved out of wood, his gaze fixed on Goliath, his heart wildly beating, while his ears drank in the vile and boastful words he uttered. At sound of his mighty voice the Israelitish troops who had been filling their water-pots at the stream-side and those who were on the fringes of the camp, fled back before him, for they were sore afraid. When David saw it, a frown gathered on his brow. He turned to those who stood near.

"Who is this accursed Philistine?" he asked them. "And how comes it that he dare insult and defy the armies of the living God? What man has been chosen to go out to meet him, and what shall be done to him when he hath laid him low, and hath washed away this shame and reproach against Israel?"

The soldiers who stood by told David that no man had yet been chosen or had dared to go out to meet the giant, but that any who accepted his challenge and met him face to face and killed him would not only be enriched with great riches but that the king himself would give him his own daughter in marriage, and from that day onward his father's whole house, whosoever he might be, would be made free men in Israel. And David hearkened, pondering what they said.

But when his eldest brother, Eliab, heard him talking, he turned on him fiercely, hot with anger. He remembered the day when the great prophet Samuel had come to Bethlehem and he himself had been set aside, and this stripling, the youngest of them all, had been blessed by the prophet and anointed with the holy oil. And he had been filled with envy when he heard that David had been summoned to court by the king.

83

"Who bade thee come idling here," he said, "leaving thy poor little flock of sheep with some herd-boy in the wilds? Oh, but I know thee of old, thy pride and presumption and the naughtiness of thy heart. Thou art puffed up with self-will, and it is not to bring a message from our father that thou hast come into the camp, but to see the fighting."

But David answered him, "What is it I have done amiss? I did but ask a question, and thou canst not deny it is one that needs an answer."

He turned away from his brother, and continued to question those who stood near, and one and all gave him the answer that had been given him already.

"But look now," he adjured them earnestly, "this boaster, monster though he be, is but a man. Weighed down with brass he moves as clumsily as an ox, and his face at least is naked. Why is he allowed to live, defying Jehovah?"

Seeing at length, though he was still little more than a boy, that David's scorn of the champion of the Philistines and his shame for Israel sprang from the courage of his very soul, these men reported the matter to their captain, who himself questioned David, and brought him to the tent of the king.

David stood beside Saul's standard while the captain went within. Then the captain led him into the tent where Saul sat, with Abner and his chief officers in attendance upon him; and David stood before the king. He bowed himself before Saul, and being questioned, said simply what was in his mind. He told the king why he had come into the camp, and how he had chanced to hear the champion of the Philistines shout his challenge against Israel, and that he had spoken only as his own soul had declared.

"Why," he said, "should any heart in Israel be faint with fear because of this man, this enemy of the Lord? Thy servant would himself go out and fight with the Philistine."

The king looked on him and marvelled, questioning within himself where he had seen his face before. But there came back no clear rememberance of the shepherd-boy who had sat beside him as he lay sick, and had solaced the dread and horror in his mind with the music of his harp.

"Of a truth," he said, "there is no doubt of thy valour. But what hope hast thou of prevailing against him? Thou art but a youth and hast had no experience in arms, while this Goliath hath been a man of war from the day when he was first able to carry a spear. He would disdain thee, my son, and snap thee in twain between his fingers."

But David pleaded with the king. He said how in days gone by, when he had sat keeping his father's sheep alone in the wild, at one time a bear and at another a young lion had sprung out from its ambush in the rocks and thickets near by, and had seized and carried off a lamb from his flock.

"So I went out after him," he said, "and chased him, and snatched his prey from out of his mouth. And when, raging with fury, he sprang upon me, his paws upon my shoulders, I caught him, like this, by the beard upon his chin, and with my club smote and slew him at a blow. So indeed, my lord, thy servant killed both the lion and the bear, and so will I do unto this accursed Philistine, for I vow, my lord, I have no fear of him, seeing that he hath defied the armies of the living God, and is himself no better than a ravening beast. The Lord God who delivered me from the paw of the lion and the paw of the bear will deliver me from the spear of this Philistine also!"

Watching David close as he stood before him and marking how his face was lit up and transfigured with the faith and courage of the spirit within him, Saul consented at length to let him go. He glanced at Abner; there was a strange influence in this young man that swept all doubts aside and prevailed over his own ripe judgement.

"Go," he said, "and may the Lord be with thee."

Then he bade his servants bring him his coat of mail and his helmet of bronze. "Thou wilt not venture out unarmed," he said.

There in the king's tent David put on Saul's coat of mail, and his helmet on his head, and girded Saul's sword about the armour as he stood. And the king with his own hand aided him. But Saul was a man of a mighty stature; and thus armed, David essayed in vain to take a pace or two, hoping that he might become accustomed to the burden, for he had never worn the like before. But he could not. He turned with a sigh to the king, and entreated that the armour should be put off him.

He said to the king: "It was in truth a grace and kindness that my lord should array me in his armour, but I cannot wear it, for I am not used to it. Be it the king's will that I go to meet Goliath as I am."

So he went out of Saul's tent with nothing in his hand but his shepherd's staff or club and his sling. When he had gone, Saul turned to Abner, the commander-in-chief of his armies, who had watched all that had passed. He asked him, "Abner, whose son is this youth?"

And Abner said: "As they soul liveth, O king, I cannot tell."

And Saul bade him make inquiry and discover from whence he came. Then the king and Abner with their officers followed after David to see what would come of his ordeal.

And David, having left the king, made his way back between the clustering tents until he had come out beyond the fringes of the camp. As he continued on his way down into the valley he came to the brook of water that flowed between the rocks in the ravine, warbling amid its stones, and gleaming in its blue in the sunbeams. It was as though he moved in a dream, but a dream marvellously clear and with all his senses alert. He stooped and chose from out of the brook's cold waters five of the smoothest pebbles on its bed, and in so doing saw the image of his own face reflected there, and it was as though he had never seen its like before. He put the pebbles into the scrip or shepherd's bag he carried, then rose and went on his way.

At the shout that had gone up from the men of Israel at sight of him, the giant who had turned back towards the Philistine camp wheeled and looked about, and knitting his shaggy eyebrows in the glare of the sun, fixed his stare on David as he rose from the brook-side and, leaping from boulder to boulder, came on down into the valley. Whereat the champion called back a word over his shoulder to his shield-bearer, and advanced to meet him.

And David, his sling in his hand, the sling with which he used to drive off the smaller beasts that pestered his flocks, drew near. The men of Israel fell silent, and the armies, clustered black on either height, watched. In the hush of the valley the skirring of the grass-hoppers in the heat of the morning, and the song of the brook-water brawling in its rocky channel, were the only sounds to be heard.

Astounded and rejoiced that after these many fruitless days there had at last come forth a man of Israel valiant enough to take up his challenge, Goliath snatched his shield from the Philistine who carried it, and stood in wait.

But when he could see his foe clearly and what manner of champion this was, little more than a lad, fair and tanned with the sun, in shepherd's clothes and unarmed, his voice pealed out in mocking laughter, and he cursed him by his gods.

"Am I a carrion dog," he cried, "that thou comest out against me with nought but a staff in thy hand? By the gods of my fathers, do but come a little closer, and I will strip the flesh from off thy body and give it to the fowls of the air, and thy bones to the wild beasts to mumble."

Even as he spoke there showed black specks in the height of the sky above the mountain-tops, and vulture and kite came

87

circling overhead against the blue above the valley.

Warily David watched the Philistine, and he stepped alertly pace with his pace and well beyond javelin cast, and circled about him so that at last he should bring the giant face to face with him against the dazzle and blaze of the sun. And as he did so, he made answer to Goliath, calling clearly across in the stillness between them.

"Thou hast come out against me, armed with sword and spear and javelin," he cried. "A brazen shield is on thine arm, and thou art hung head to foot with armour of brass. But if this be all thy strength, beware of it! For I am come out against thee in the name of the Lord of Hosts, the God of the armies of Israel, whom thou hast insulted and defied, and this day the Lord will deliver thee into my hand. And I will smite thee and take thy head from off thy shoulders, and not only thy carcass but the carcasses of the host of the Philistines shall be given this day to the fowls of the air and the beasts of the wild. That all the earth may know there is a God in Israel, and that his salvation is not in sword and spear, nor his battle to the strong, but that he giveth victory according as he decree."

In rage and fury at these words, Goliath raised himself, towering in his might, his blood roaring in his ears, and with lifted spear strode in to smite his enemy down, and his armour clanged as he trod.

And David drew back lightly from before him. He watched every transient look upon the great flushed bony countenance beneath the crested helmet, now full in the glare of noonday. And softly as he sped on, he drew from out of his scrip one after another of the pebbles he had chosen from the brook and poised it in his sling. His first stone rang out sharp upon the champion's breastplate; and the next numbed the hand that held his spear; for David could sling a stone at a hair-breadth, and not miss.

Then of a sudden he turned swiftly, and with the speed of an angel sent from God, ran in towards the giant, whirling his sling above his head as he did so, his gaze fixed gravely on the target of his face. And as he looked, Goliath's heart fainted within him and he was cold as stone. He stood bemused. And David lifted his thumb, set free the stone, and slang it straight at its mark. It whistled through the air, and smote the Philistine in the middle of his forehead, clean between the eyes. The stone sank into his forehead, and into his brain and, without a groan, the giant fell stunned upon his face upon the ground. The noise of his fall was like the clashing of innumerable cymbals, and the dust above his body rose over him in a cloud.

Before he could stir from the swoon in which he lay, David ran and stood over him. And with his two hands he drew the giant's bronze two-bladed sword from out of its sheath, wheeled it with all his might above his shoulders and at a blow smote off Goliath's head.

Then with his two hands he snatched up the helmetless matted head and held it high aloft before all Israel. And there went up a cry.

When the Philistines, who had been watching the combat from the heights above, saw that their champion had been defeated and lay prone, dead, and headless upon the ground they fled in terror back towards their camp. A wild clamour arose as the news of the champion's downfall sped on from mouth to mouth; cries of astonishment and fear.

Then sounded the trumpets in the camp of Israel. The Lord had wrought a great salvation, and the men of Israel and the men of Judah, shouting their war cry, swept down into the valley and up the slopes beyond, and stormed the heights of Shochoh. Rank on rank they pressed forward, beating down all resistance, and the Philistine army broke and fled. Westward and north-westward the Israelites pursued them through the valleys and ravines until they came out on to the plain and even to the walls of Ekron and of Gath. Throughout the whole way to Shaaraim the ground was strewn with their dead and wounded, to the very gates of the two cities.

Thence the pursuers turned back. And when they had come from chasing after the Philistines, they plundered their tents, a rich booty. Laden with their spoil, they returned to their own camp. And the armour of Goliath was stripped from his body, and with his spear, his javelin and his sword, was afterwards laid up as a trophy in Jerusalem.

When David himself returned from the pursuit of the Philistines he was brought to Abner, and Abner himself took him into the presence of Saul. And Jonathan was with his father the king. David came in and stood before them, the head of the Philistine in his hand. Saul looked from the one face, wan and swarthy and dark and shut by death, to the other, young and bright with life and aware, and he marvelled.

He asked David whose son he was, and many other questions. David told him that he was the son of Jesse of Bethlehem. And there returned into Saul's mind, as though it were a dream that had faded out after waking, the memory of the hours when he had lain terrified and distraught in the gloom of his tent, and his only solace had been the music of David's harp-strings.

He said nothing of it, but talked long and earnestly with him, and questioned him. And David answered the king simply and openly, while Jonathan who had been absent from his father during his sickness, stood near at hand, his eyes fixed on David's face, as he mutely drank in every word he uttered. His heart welled over with wonder at his simplicity and fearlessness, and his soul went out to David. He loved him—as do all men who love—at first sight. And he continued to love him, friend with friend, until the last hour of his life.

So great was the love of Jonathan for David that he made a covenant of brotherhood with him, a covenant that in Israel knitted two friends together in mind and spirit closer even than if they had been sons of the same mother.

"Whatever thy soul desireth, that will I indeed do for thee," he said. And in token of it he stripped himself of the cloak which he wore, a cloak befitting the son of a king, and he gave it to David, and his armour also, even to his sword and his bow. And he girdled him with his girdle.

From that day forward Saul took David into his service and made him his armour-bearer, and David returned no more to the house of his father.

When the king, with his captains and his army, laden with the spoil they had taken from the Philistines, returned in triumph from their camp above the valley of Elah and marched to Gibeah, a vast concourse of people gathered together to watch them pass.

And the women and maidens of Israel, clad in their brightest colours, scarlet and blue and purple, came out singing and dancing from all the towns and villages on their way to meet and greet King Saul, and to give him welcome.

To the clash of timbrel and of cymbal and the music of divers instruments they came dancing in two companies, scattering garlands before the king, singing his praises; and as the one company chanted their song of victory, so the other answered them again, shrill and wild and sweet; and the refrain of their song was:

"Saul hath slain his thousands, but David hath slain his tens of thousands."

And Saul's heart sank within him. The words displeased him, and he thought, "To David they have given ten times the praise that they have given to me. What more is wanting to his glory than the kingdom itself?"

From that day forward he was filled with envy of David and looked at him askance. Nevertheless, to the joy and satisfaction

91

of the people and of his own officers, Saul made him the captain of a thousand.

And David was renowned and beloved throughout Israel, for he bore himself wisely in all his ways, and the Lord was with him.

The Giant who had no Heart in his Body

A Scandinavian Story

Retold by Gwyn Jones

The basic theme of the giant who hides his heart and replaces it with one of stone so that no one can kill him occurs in folktales from many European countries. The different versions vary widely, and this one from Scandinavia is one of the best.

Once upon a time, and a time before that, there was a King who had seven sons, and as no king had ever sons finer, so no king had such love for his sons as he. He more than loved, he doted on them, and morning and noon, by twilight and dark, there was always a son with him, for he could not bear to let them out of his sight all seven together. And if there was any change as the years rolled by, it was that he doted on them still more fondly. That was how it happened that when at last they asked his leave to go a-wooing—and they grown lads, with down on their lips, and golden razors, too—he insisted that one of them must stay behind and keep him company. To the six eldest this sounded reasonable enough, and as for the youngest—well, he was the youngest, wasn't he? Besides, they promised to bring him back a

Princess as lovely as their own.

Because he doted on his six fine sons, the King gave them the handsomest wooing suits that mortal ever saw, with scarlet silks and golden cord and pins of the whitest silver. Kingfisher-bright on rainbow horses they rode away, to palaces and castles by river and mountain and sea, till at last they came to a King who had six daughters, their hair yellower than the primrose, and their throats whiter than milk. Of all the Princesses they had ever seen these were the loveliest; they instantly fell to wooing them, and it is soonest to say that their wooing prospered, and they were to take them home as sweethearts; and so they did, and loved them so deeply that they quite forgot they had promised to take home for their youngest brother Agnar a Princess as lovely as their own.

Woodpecker-bright and primrose-ladied they were making their way home when they passed a big hard house like a steep hard hill. Now who should be living there but a giant, and when he heard such youthful joy and laughter, "I'll soon put an end to that!" he said, and did, for he just gave them one of his stares, and they were all turned to stone, and stayed there motionless just outside his garden.

Meantime the King was waiting for his six sons, but the longer he waited the longer he had to, with no sound or savour of them, till at last he feared he should never see his darlings again.

"If I had not you left," he told Agnar, "I should put an end to my life, for no man was ever so unhappy as I when I think of your poor dear brothers."

"That reminds me, Father," said Agnar. "I have been thinking to go and look for them, and look for my Princess too."

"Princess!" scolded his father. "How can you think of such trifles when your poor dear brothers may be lying dead, dazed, or hurt, for all we know!"

"That is just what I want to find out," Agnar comforted him, "so you may as well say yes now as later."

At last say yes he did. But he had spent so many guineas on fitting out his eldest that he had not one milled penny to spare for his youngest; and when Agnar rode off it was in rough trousers and a leather jacket, on a broken-winded pot-bellied nag that looked as though it had been cut out of a hedge with a bread-knife, and someone stoutly defending the hedge while it happened. Not that Agnar cared. He leaped on his steed with a cheer.

"Good-bye, Father," he called. "I'll be back, never fear, and my six brothers with me, and a Princess with yellow hair into the bargain."

He had ridden only a short road when he came across a Raven lying on the hard ground and hardly able to lift a feather, it was so thin and starved.

"Help me, dear friend," croaked the Raven. "Give me a little food, and in your own hour of need you will not regret it."

"I am short of food myself," said Prince Agnar, "and I can't imagine what help a Raven can give me. Still, your need *is* great, so here you are, friend: eat up."

He had ridden only a short road further when he had to cross a brook, and there in the brook lay a Salmon which had got into a dry place and was thrashing about in despair.

"Help me, dear friend," panted the Salmon. "Put me into the water again, and in your own hour of need you will not regret it."

"I can't imagine what help a Salmon can give me," said Prince Agnar, "but I won't see you lie there and choke." And with a quick heave he put him back in the water.

This time he rode quite a long road before he met a Wolf, crawling along the hard ground on its belly, it was so thin and weak and famished.

"Help me, dear friend," moaned the Wolf, "and give me your horse. It is two years since I last had a square meal, and every time I breathe I whistle."

"Just a minute," said Prince Agnar. "First I come to a Raven, and I have to give him my food. Next I come to a Salmon, and have to heave him back into the water. And now I come to a Wolf, who wants to eat my horse. It can't be done, Wolf, you must see that: for then I should have nothing to ride on."

"Yes, you would," pleaded the Wolf. "You can ride on me, and in your own hour of need you will not regret it."

"I can't imagine what help a Wolf can give me," said Agnar, "but I won't see you starve: eat away."

When the Wolf had done eating, Agnar took the bit and slipped it between his jaws, and laid the saddle over his back, and mounted. The Wolf was so big and strong after all he had tucked inside him that the Prince seemed no more than a hair on his back, and they travelled like the wind.

"A bit further on," said the Wolf, "I will show you the Giant's house. Ah, there it is, and here are your six brothers and their six brides, whom the Giant has turned to stone; and there is the door of the house, and that is the way you must now go."

"Won't he turn me to stone too?" asked Agnar.

"Not if you take my advice. For when you get inside you will find a Princess there, and she will tell you how to kill the Giant. Just be careful to do everything she orders."

Off went the Wolf, and in went the Prince, and it would be silly to pretend that he was anything but afraid. Luckily, the Giant was away just then; but the Princess was at home, as the Wolf had said; and of all princesses in the world she was the loveliest, with long, long hair yellower than the primrose, and her throat whiter than milk.

"Heaven help you!" cried the Princess as he came in. "Flee at once or nothing can save you."

Agnar had much the same notion, but for the Princess's sake he put a bold face on it and asked where was the Giant, for he had come to kill him.

"There is no chance of that," lamented the Princess, "for he has no heart in his body. So flee before he returns from the forest."

Agnar thought that no bad idea, but for the Princess's sake he put another bold face on and said that since he had come so far he must try to free his brothers, who stood outside turned to stone along with their primrose brides. "And I should like to free *you*, Princess, most of all. So have you a plan?"

"Of a kind," she told him. "You must creep in under the bed and listen to everything the Giant and I may say. But if you are not quieter than a mouse, he will soon have the skin off your toes."

Agnar thought that only too likely, but he crept in under the bed, and had just made himself comfortable when the Giant came clumping in.

"Ha," roared the giant, and "Ho! What a smell of Christian blood is here!"

"What a good nose you have, Giant," said the Princess, "for a magpie flew over the house with a man's bone in its bill and dropped it down the chimney, and that is the smell you smell."

"That makes one magpie," said the Giant, and ate a roast sheep, and when it was night-time they went to bed.

After a while Agnar heard the Princess say: "Giant, are you asleep?"

"No," he said. "Why?"

"Because there is one thing I so want to ask you, if only I dared."

"What was that?" he asked.

"Where do you keep the heart that isn't in your body?"

"Mind your own business," roared the Giant. "Still if you must know, it lies under the door-sill."

"Ha, ha," said Agnar to himself under the bed. "We'll soon

see about that."

The next morning the Giant was hardly inside the forest before Agnar held a pick and the Princess a shovel; but dig and hunt as they might there was no heart there. "What it is to be tied to a liar," said the Princess. "Still, we must try him once more."

To cover up their digging she gathered all the prettiest flowers she could find and strewed them over the replaced door-sill. Then Agnar crept in under the bed again, and had just made himself comfortable when the Giant came bumping in.

"Fy," roared the Giant, and "Faugh! What a smell of Christian flesh is here!"

"What happened yesterday can happen to-day," said the Princess. "A second magpie flew over the house with a man's bone and dropped it down our chimney."

"That makes two of them," said the Giant, and ate a roast goat, and when it was night-time they went to bed.

After a while Agnar heard the Giant say: "Princess, are you sleeping?"

"No," she said. "Why?"

"Because I wanted to ask you who strewed flowers all over the door-sill."

"It was I," said the Princess prettily, "and the reason was that I am so fond of you that I just couldn't help it once I knew your heart lay there."

"Goose!" roared the Giant. "It doesn't lie there at all."

"Oh," she replied. "Where does it lie, then?"

"In the cupboard on the wall," he told her.

"Ho, ho," said Agnar to himself under the bed. "We'll soon see about that."

The next morning the Giant was hardly out through the door before Agnar held a knife and the Princess a gimlet; but probe and scrape as they might there was no heart there. "We must try

him once more," said the Princess.

To cover up their searching she decked out the cupboard with the prettiest flowers she could find; Agnar crept in under the bed again, and just as he was comfortable the Giant came thumping in.

"Ugh," roared the Giant, and "Urgh! What a smell of Christian bones is here!"

"A magpie flew over the house with a man's bone in its bill and dropped it down our chimney," said the Princess. "What a good nose you have, Giant!"

"That makes three of them," said the Giant, and ate a roast ox, and when it was night-time they went to bed.

After a while Agnar heard the Giant ask who had decked the cupboard with flowers, and why.

"It was I," said the Princess prettily, "and the reason I did it is that I am fond of you I just couldn't stop myself once I knew your heart lay there."

"Goose and ducky!" roared the Giant. "It doesn't lie there at all."

"Where does it lie, then?" she asked.

"Where you will never come to it," he retorted.

Even so, she told him, it would be a great comfort and pleasure to her to know where his heart lay safe and warm and free from harm, and she kept on at him till the Giant could hold out no longer, and what Agnar then heard him say was this:

"Far, far away, in a forest stands a lake; in that lake lies an island; in that island stands a church; in that church lies a well; in that well swims a duck; in that duck abides an egg, and in that egg there lies my heart—you fond and faithful darling!"

"Heigh-ho," said Agnar to himself under the bed. "We'll soon see about that."

The next morning at dawn the Giant was off to the forest. "And I must be off too," said Agnar, "if only I knew how and where." He looked out of doors and there was the Wolf with his bit and saddle waiting for him.

"How has it gone?" the Wolf asked him, and he told him his story down to the last small syllable. "Jump on," said the Wolf. "I'll soon find a way." And when Agnar had taken a long farewell of the Princess they went off like the wind. The heavens hissed, the earth rattled, the trees went swish-swish-swish at their passage, and in just three days they reached the lake in the forest. Now Prince Agnar could not swim, because his father had never trusted all his sons in the water together, but, "Hold tight," said the Wolf, and he crossed that lake as though his toes were webbed. In this way they reached the island and rode to the church, but the church keys were hanging high at the top of an un-climbable tower, and Agnar felt as far from the Giant's heart as ever.

"It is now time to call on the Raven," said the Wolf.

When he had called but once, twice, thrice, there was the Raven circling high above them and coming in to land, then back up again to the church tower, and down to lay the keys in Agnar's hand. And there inside the church they found the well, and in the well swam the duck, backwards and forwards, forwards and backwards, in the trickiest manner imaginable. For a long time he stood there coaxing it, and now it was almost in his grasp, and then out and away, till finally it paddled right up to him and he was able to seize it. But even as he was lifting it out of the water it dropped the egg into the well, and Agnar was frantic with anxiety as to how he might get it out again.

"It is now time to call on the Salmon," said the Wolf.

When he had called but once, twice, thrice, there was the Salmon swimming far below them and coming up to the surface, then back down again to the bottom of the well, and up once more to place the egg in Agnar's hand.

"What now?" asked Agnar. The Wolf said, "Give it a

101

squeeze," and as Agnar did so they heard the Giant scream. "Squeeze it again," said the Wolf, and the Giant screamed worse than ever, and they heard him babbling and promising to do anything the Prince asked, if only he would not squeeze his heart in two.

"Tell him he must restore your brothers to life again, and the six primrose ladies whom he turned into stone. And tell him to be quick about it," said the Wolf.

It was no sooner said than done, and the six stone brothers became king's sons again, and the six stone sisters king's daughters.

"What now?" asked Agnar.

"Squeeze the egg in two!" howled the Wolf, and that is exactly what he did, and as the egg burst in pieces the Giant burst in pieces too, with a loud, harmonious report.

And when the sound of it had died down, and the birds were settling to the boughs, the Prince said thank you to the Raven and the Salmon, and rode back to the Giant's house on his friend the Wolf. There stood his six brothers alive and merry, and their brides all milky-throated. Then Agnar went into the house to find his Princess, and if she was lovely when first he saw her, she was ten times lovelier now. So off they rode, goldfinch-bright and primrose-ladied, till they reached the old King's castle. He laughed till he wept, and wept till he laughed, and sometimes he laughed and wept together, such was his joy at their returning. And when the brothers sat to table, by the vote of them all Agnar sat at their head, and his Princess sat beside him. And so they lived, and so they loved, and with Black-wing the Raven, and Silver-scale the Salmon, and good old Grey-legs the Wolf, saw the sun down the sky for many a golden year. When the old King died it was Agnar and his bride who succeeded to the kingdom, and when last we heard of them, why, they were still on the throne and living happily ever after.

Strong Gottlieb

A German Story

By Ludwig Bechstein
Translated by Anthea Bell

Ludwig Bechstein, nineteenth-century poet and scholar, was an inde-
fatigable collector of folktales. Told at the fireside, and full of all the
familiar and traditional characters, these tales were handed down by word
of mouth for generations. In this story, Strong Gottlieb outwits a greedy
landowner who doesn't want to pay a decent wage.

There was once a rich gentleman who had a great many men
working on his land. One of them, who proved himself to be a
particularly faithful servant, had a fine boy born to him. The
gentleman promised to take the child into his service, too, if he
grew really strong. The boy's father remembered his promise.
He was determined to make his son—whom he named Gottlieb
—grow really strong. For seven years, he gave the boy nothing
but milk to drink, and nothing but meat to eat, so that Gottlieb
grew big and strong.

When seven years were up, the man took his son Gottlieb to

the landowner. "Look at this fine boy, master!" said he. "He's strong for his age already."

There was a young tree growing in the garden where the father and son were talking to the gentleman, and the master said, "Pull up this tree, Gottlieb!"

However, Gottlieb could not pull up the tree, so the gentleman said, "The boy's still too young and weak. It would be too much to expect him to do heavy work yet."

So the man took his son away again, and, for seven years more gave him milk to drink and meat to eat. When the seven years were up, he took his son back to the landowner again. Gottlieb looked strong enough for work, but first, the gentleman wanted him to work for a day on trial. By now, what with his own sturdy frame and his strengthening diet, Gottlieb had grown so very strong that, to show what he could do, he immediately pulled up a great stout tree with his little finger. This frightened everyone. The gentleman's wife in particular was afraid of such strength, and she could not stand the sight of Gottlieb.

Gottlieb found his first day's work quite easy.

At dinner time the maid servant carried in a dish of potatoes and buttermilk and went to call the other farm hands. Meanwhile Gottlieb, who had finished his work first, began eating. Soon the dish was empty.

When the other men came in for their dinner, Gottlieb got up from the chimney corner where he had been sitting, scratched his head and said, "There was some food here, but it wasn't much. I thought it was all for me, so I ate it up."

Gottlieb's huge appetite appalled the others, and they gave their voracious companion black looks.

After dinner, they went out threshing. In Gottlieb's hands the flail was at light as a feather. He threw it in the air and caught it coming down, as boys catch sticks. Then he tore out a tree for a flail, and threshed so hard that the corn was ground to flour on the spot. The straw was cut into chaff, and it was all beaten right into the ground. This was going too far for his master's liking. He was alarmed to see what a dangerous servant he had, and wondered how best to get rid of him. So he asked Gottlieb what wages he wanted. Gottlieb went over to the gentleman and whispered something in his ear. At that the gentleman turned red. "Very well," said he, "but not a word!" And he took Gottlieb on as a farmhand, which did not please the other men at all.

The landowner was very greedy and grasping, and liked to keep wages as low as possible. Gottlieb, who did not see why he had to grow so strong just to work for others, knew that.

When the gentleman was alone with his wife, she asked him what wages Gottlieb wanted.

"Why, my dear!" said he. "I will never get such a strong worker so cheap! Gottlieb wants no wages at all!"

"None at all? That's impossible!" cried his wife in amazement. "There's something behind this! Husband, you are not telling me that truth!"

"No, no, don't distress yourself, dear wife!" the gentleman reassured her. "He does want something, and I've promised it to him, but it won't cost a penny. Only it must be kept a close secret between us."

"A secret between us!" replied his wife. "Well, you must tell me what it is first!"

"Gottlieb is going to give me something when the year is up!" stammered the landowner.

"Give you something? What can your servant's son give you?" asked his wife.

"Well, it's a box," replied her husband, "that's what he's going to give me."

"A box! Husband, you're out of your mind!" cried the woman, getting angry. "And where does he think to find this box?"

105

"Oh, there are plenty of those around," replied the land-owner. "Gottlieb means a box on the ear."

"Oh, you fool!" cried his wife in horror. "That's what comes of all your avarice! You'd rather be disgraced than pay a decent wage. Gottlieb will kill you; where he strikes the ground, grass never grows again. Oh, what a terrible bargain! But leave everything to me; I'll save you. I'll soon get rid of him!"

"Well, if you can get rid of him, my dear," said the gentleman meekly, "I've no objection at all."

So the gentleman's wife made a plan. There was a haunted mill on the estate; many people had been strangled by the hobgoblin that lived there.

"Gottlieb, you are to take four bushels of corn to the mill and grind them!" she told the new farmhand, one day.

"Just as you say, mistress!" answered Gottlieb. He took a big sack, filled it with eight bushels of corn, threw it over his shoulder and went off to the mill, whistling cheerfully. When he came to the mill the door was closed. Gottlieb knocked politely —once, twice, three times. As no one opened the door he pushed it a little with his foot, and the door burst open, splitting in two. The millstones lay in Gottlieb's path, so he just kicked them aside, to the left and to the right of him, and went into the mill.

Before unloading the corn and beginning to work he lit a fire, made himself some soup and put a bit of ham into it. Up came a big cat with burning eyes. She opened her mouth wide, glared at strong Gottlieb and cried, "Miaow!"

"Shoo, cat!" said Gottlieb, giving her such a push that she ran off in a hurry. Then he poured the corn out of the sack, set the mill going, and ate his breakfast.

Back came the cat again, spitting and miaowing.

"Shoo, cat!" cried Gottlieb again, throwing the ham bone at her head. It whirled her around and around, and she disappeared.

Suddenly a terrible giant appeared before strong Gottlieb. "Who said you could grind corn here, mealworm?" he bellowed.

Gottlieb immediately took a millstone and threw it at the giant's forehead. "Who said you could boast and brag here, millworm?" said he. The giant fell over backward with such a howl that the whole mill shook. As for Gottlieb, he put the flour in his sack, put the bran in a second sack, and took them both home.

"Heaven help us!" wailed the gentleman's wife. "The scoundrel's alive and he's coming back again."

But soon she thought of a new trick. "The well needs cleaning!" she said the next day. "The water tastes foul and muddy. Gottlieb can climb down and do the job."

And she said secretly to the other men, "When he's down the well, take good care you don't let any stones fall from the rim of the well, and land on the head of that guzzler who eats up all your dinners!"

The farmhands understood what she meant, and when Gottlieb was down the well they threw down stones on him from above. The stones rattled and plopped into the deep well, and some of them fell on strong Gottlieb.

"You fools up there!" shouted Gottlieb. "Who's shaking sand into this inkwell? Just wait until I come up again; I'll show you a thing or two!"

Hearing this, the men ran away in a fright and hid, and Gottlieb climbed out of the well like a chimney sweep out of a chimney.

The gentleman's wife was now at her wit's end, wondering how to get rid of strong Gottlieb. Then she remembered that there was an enchanted castle high up on top of the mountain, a very strange place, indeed. It was haunted by the ghost of an old giant who had done wicked things in ancient times, and had been doomed to haunt this castle. Moreover, the giant had cheated the ancestors of the present landowner shamefully when he sold the estate to them long ago.

The gentleman's wife sent Gottlieb to the castle. She spoke to him with false friendliness, telling him that the previous owner of the land lived there, and that he owed her husband a lot of money. If Gottlieb brought the money home, she said, he could keep part of it for himself. So Gottlieb left at once.

Soon, he came to the top of the mountain. He was very much surprised. "Hm!" said he to himself, "down there they kept on saying this was a ruined old castle, but this is a fine, brand-new house! There must be plenty of money here!"

He came to the gate of the fine building, and as there was no bellpush he knocked at the door. But it stayed shut fast.

"This is ridiculous!" muttered Gottlieb. "I'll just have to open the door myself." And he pushed the door a little with his foot. With that, the whole building shook, and the door burst wide open with a sound like a clap of thunder. But as soon as Gottlieb went inside, he was surrounded by a crowd of ghosts, led by the terrible giant at whom Gottlieb had thrown the millstone in the mill.

"Aha! An old acquaintance!" said Gottlieb. "Can you be Master Paynought, who steals other men's money? Just bring it out, will you!"

"What's that you say, you wretched little creature?" the giant bellowed, making horrible faces. "Just you wait, whipper-snapper!"

"Oho! We'll see about that!" cried Gottlieb. He wrenched out one of a pair of double doors and flung it at the giant's forehead, where the scar left by the millstone was still visible. He hurled the second door after the first, and now the giant ran off as fast as he could go, throwing a sack full of money at Gottlieb. Gottlieb caught it and went away with it at once.

The master was delighted with the sack of money that

Gottlieb brought home, but he still wished to get rid of the strong man. He was horribly frightened of that box on the ear. So he arranged with his shepherd to take the blow in return for a sum of money. The gentleman then called his men together—all but Gottlieb—and told them he was sending them to the forest next day to chop wood. They must come home in good time, and the last one arriving would be dismissed from his service—and he wouldn't be too angry if Gottlieb were the last home. This suited the men perfectly. Early next morning, they all hurried off to chop wood, and one of them awoke Gottlieb.

When Gottlieb turned up at last, still drowsy, and rubbing his eyes, his master cried, "Why, lazybones, all the others are chopping wood already, and the man who comes home last will be dismissed!"

"What?" cried Gottlieb, stretching and yawning. "That's the first I heard of it! Well, here goes, then!" And he took his axe, and off he went to the wood.

Gottlieb met his fellow servants on their way back from work. Quickly, he ran back to a big lake which had recently been made. A footbridge over its outlet was the only way from the wood to the gentleman's estate. He pulled open the floodgates, so that all the water flowed out into a broad channel, kicked down the bridge and let the planks float away on the water. Then he went, at a leisurely pace, to meet the other farmhands. They were laughing spitefully at him, happy to think that he was going to be dismissed that very day.

"Don't be in too much of a hurry!" said Gottlieb. "Wait a minute, and I'll soon be back." And off he went to the wood.

Meanwhile, the farmhands came to the torrent of water foaming by, with no way across. So they just had to wait until Gottlieb came back again. Gottlieb had easily done a day's work in less than an hour. He had a hay pole with him. He planted it in the river and swung himself over to the opposite bank. Then he threw it back over the water and called to his companions, "Do as I do!" However, they could not lift the hay pole even two at a time, so they were forced to stay where they were until the lake was empty, which took more than a day.

By this time, the landowner was desperately anxious to get rid of Gottlieb, and he now offered to pay him his wages. He told Gottlieb that he had found someone else to take the blow, and after that Gottlieb could go where he liked and stay where he pleased.

"Well," said Gottlieb, "let's put it to the trial. I was on trial myself."

Up came the shepherd. Gottlieb looked pityingly at him, and said with a smile, "You? You want to take my blow?" He lifted him up, and struck him in the face so hard that the shepherd flew through the air like a ball. When the gentleman and his wife saw what had happened they crossed themselves, and were thankful that it had not been the gentleman himself who took the blow.

"There, Gottlieb!" they said. "You can go now!"

"Go?" said Gottlieb. "Dear me, no; I don't care to do that. In any case, I can't go; the shepherd was not the right man. It was you who hired me, master. You said I could go where I liked and stay where I pleased, didn't you?"

"Yes, indeed I did!" snapped the gentleman. "What more do you want of me?"

"Why, then," replied Gottlieb, "I'm going to my bed, and I'll stay here on your estate as long as I please!"

The gentleman was furious. "Curse you, stay then!" he cried. "I'll go! I'm not living near you any longer. I might find myself flying through the air one of these fine days, like soap bubbles or a shooting star. Take it all, and much good may it do you!"

Quite beside themselves with rage and fury, the gentleman and his wife went away as fast as they could. As for Gottlieb, he hired the men and maidservants himself, had his old mother brought to the gentleman's house and gave her a golden bed with silk sheets and pillows. Every day she had the best wine to drink, and all sorts of good things to eat, and she lived in the lap of luxury, like a great lady.

The Magic Feather

A Dakota Indian Tale

By Margaret Compton

In the folklore of the American Indians imaginary characters were used to portray events that actually took place in history. Giants always represented a strong enemy tribe or an evil threat. In most folktales good overcomes evil and the giant is the loser. In this unusual story it is the giant who comes out on top.

In the depths of the forest in the land of the Dacotahs stood a wigwam many leagues distant from any other. The old man who had been known to live in it was supposed to have died; but he kept himself in hiding for the sake of his little grandson, whose mother had brought him there to escape the giants.

The Dacotahs had once been a brave and mighty people. They were swift runners and proud of their fleetness. It had been told among the nations for many generations that a great chief should spring from this tribe, and that he should conquer all his enemies, even the giants who had made themselves strong by eating the flesh of those they took in battle and drinking their blood. This great chief should wear a white feather and should be known by its name.

112

The giants believed the story and sought to prevent it coming true. So they said to the Dacotahs: "Let us run a race. If you win you shall have our sons and our daughters to do with them as you please, and if we win we will take yours."

Some of the wise Indians shook their heads and said: "Suppose the giants win; they will kill our children and will serve them as dainty food upon their tables." But the young men answered: "Kaw: who can outrun the Dacotahs? We shall return from the race with the young giants bound hand and foot, to fetch and carry for us all our days." So they agreed to the wager and ran with the giants.

Now, it was not to be supposed that the giants would act fairly. They dug pitfalls on the prairie, covering them with leaves and grass, which caused the runners to stumble, and lose the race.

The Dacotahs, therefore, had to bring out their children and give them to the giants. But when they were counted one child was missing. The giants roared with anger and made the whole tribe search for him, but he could not be found. Then the giants killed the father instead and ate his flesh, grumbling and muttering vengeance with every mouthful.

This was the boy whose home was in the forest. When he was still a very little fellow his grandfather had made him a tiny bow and some smooth, light arrows, and taught him how to use them.

The first time he ventured from the lodge he brought home a rabbit, the second time a squirrel, and he shot a fine, large deer long before he was strong enough to drag it home.

One day when he was about fourteen years old, he heard a voice calling to him as he went through the thick woods: "Come hither, you wearer of the white feather. You do not yet wear it, but you are worthy of it."

He looked about, but at first saw no one. At last he caught sight of the head of a little old man among the trees. On going up

113

to it he discovered that the body from the heart downwards was wood and fast in the earth. He thought some hunter must have leaped upon a rotten stump and, it giving way, had caught and held him fast; but he soon recognized the roots of an old oak that he well knew. Its top had been blighted by a stroke of lightning, and the lower branches were so dark that no birds built their nests on them, and few even lighted upon them.

The boy knew nothing of the world except what his grandfather had taught him. He had once found some lodge poles on the edge of the forest and a heap of ashes like those about their own wigwam, by which he guessed that there were other people living. He had never been told why he was living with an old man so far away from others, or of his father, but the time had come for him to know these things.

The head which had called him, said as he came near: "Go home, White Feather, and lie down to sleep. You will dream, and on waking will find a pipe, a pouch of smoking mixture, and a long white feather beside you. Put the feather on your head, and as you smoke you will see the cloud which rises from your pipe pass out of the doorway as a flock of pigeons."

The voice then told him who he was, and also that the giants had never given up looking for him. He was to wait for them no longer, but to go boldly to their lodge and offer to race with them. "Here," said the voice, "is an enchanted vine which you are to throw over the head of everyone who runs with you."

White Feather, as he was thenceforth called, picked up the vine, went quickly home and did as he had been told. He heard the voice, awoke and found the pouch of tobacco, the pipe, and the white feather. Placing the feather on his head, he filled the pipe and sat down to smoke.

His grandfather, who was at work not far from the wigwam, was astonished to see flocks of pigeons flying over his head, and still more surprised to find that they came from his own

doorway. When he went in and saw the boy wearing the white feather, he knew what it all meant and became very sad, for he loved the boy so much that he could not bear the thought of losing him.

The next morning White Feather went in search of the giants. He passed through the forest, out upon the prairie and through other woods across another prairie, until at last he saw a tall lodge pole in the middle of the forest. He went boldly up to it, thinking to surprise the giants, but his coming was not unexpected, for the little spirits which carry the news had heard the voice speaking to the boy and had hastened to tell those whom it most concerned.

The giants were six brothers who lived in a lodge that was ill-kept and dirty. When they saw the boy approaching they made fun of him among themselves; but when he entered the lodge they pretended that they were glad to see him and flattered him, telling him that his fame as a brave had already reached them.

White Feather knew well what they wanted. He proposed the race; and though this was just what they had intended doing, they laughed at his offer. At last they said that if this was his wish he should try first with the smallest and weakest of their number.

They were to run towards the east until they came to a certain well-known tree which had been stripped of its bark, and then back to the starting point, where a war-club made of iron was driven into the ground. Whoever reached this first was to beat the other's brains out with it.

White Feather and the youngest giant ran nimbly on, and the giants, who were watching, were rejoicing to see their brother gain slowly but surely, and at last shoot ahead of White Feather.

When his enemy was almost at the goal, the boy, who was only a few feet behind, threw the enchanted vine over the giant's head, which caused him to fall back helpless. No one suspected anything more than an accident, for the vine could not be seen except by him who carried it.

After White Feather had cut off the giant's head, the brothers feeling sure they could get the better of him, begged him to leave the head with them, for they thought that by magic they might bring it back to life. But the boy claimed his right to take it home to his grandfather.

The next morning he returned to run with the second giant, whom he defeated in the same manner; the third morning the third, and so on until all but one was killed.

As he marched towards the giant's lodge on the sixth morning he heard the voice of the old man of the oak tree who had first appeared to him. It came to warn him. It told him that the sixth giant was afraid to race with him, and instead would therefore try to deceive him and work enchantment on him.

As he went through the wood, the voice continued, White Feather would meet a beautiful woman—the most beautiful in the world. To avoid danger he must wish himself to be an elk and he would be changed into that animal. Even then he must keep out of her way, for she meant to do him harm.

White Feather had not gone far from the tree when he met her. He had never seen a woman before, and this one was so beautiful that he wished himself an elk at once, for he was sure she would bewitch him. He could not tear himself away from the spot, however, but kept browsing near her, raising his eyes now and then to look at her.

She went to him, laid her hand upon his neck and stroked his sides. Looking from him she sighed, and as he turned his head towards her, she reproached him for changing himself from a tall and handsome man to such an ugly creature. "For," said she, "I heard of you in a distant land, and, though many sought me, I came hither to be your wife."

As White Feather looked at her he saw tears shining in her

117

eyes, and almost before he knew it he wished himself a man again. In a moment he was restored to his natural shape, and the woman flung her arms about his neck and kissed him, and by and by she coaxed him to lie down on the ground and put his head on her lap.

Now, this beautiful woman was really the giant in disguise; and as White Feather lay with his head on her knee, she stroked his hair and forehead, and by her magic put him to sleep. Then she took an axe and broke his back. This done, she changed herself into the giant, turned White Feather into a dog, and bade him follow to the lodge.

The giant took the white feather and placed it on his head, for he knew there was magic in it; and he wished to make the tribes honour him as the great warrior they had long expected.

Thor's Wonderful Journey

By M.W. Mabie

The Norsemen were a nation of bold warriors who admired the qualities of strength and bravery above all things. The traditional stories they told were about their gods: the mighty Odin, who ruled all; Thor, the god of Thunder; and Loki, the mischief-maker. Every Norseman longed to be like the gods—eternally striving against their adversaries who dwelled in the grim northern mountains. Share the exciment of Thor's Wonderful Journey, *as he tests his strength and skill against the magical, mystical powers of the King of the Giants!*

Thor made many journeys and had many strange adventures; but there was one journey which was more wonderful than all the others, and which proves, moreover, that the strongest and truest are sometimes deceived by those who are weaker than themselves. The giants in old Norse times were not easy to conquer; but generally it was when they hid themselves behind lies and appeared to be what they were not they succeeded for a time. Thor's strength was a noble thing because he used it to help men; but his truthfulness and honesty were nobler still.

One morning, just as the sun was beginning to shine through

119

the mists that overhung the world, the gates of Asgard opened and Thor's chariot, drawn by the goats, rattled along the road. Thor and Loki were evidently off for a journey; but Thor was always going off somewhere, and nobody who saw him now thought that he was starting out to try his strength with the most powerful things in the whole earth. Nor did he know it.

All day long the chariot rolled across the level stretches of meadow and through the valleys, leaving the echoes shouting to each other from the overhanging mountains as it passed by. At night it stopped at the house of a poor peasant, and Thor stepped down and stood in the doorway.

"Can you lodge two travellers overnight?" he asked.

"Certainly," said the peasant, "but we can give you nothing to eat, for we have nothing for ourselves."

"Give yourselves no trouble about that," answered Thor cheerfully. "I can provide for all."

He went back to Loki, who got out of the chariot; and then, to the great astonishment of the people in the house, Thor killed both his goats, and in a minute they were ready for cooking. The great pot was soon sending savoury odours through the house, and the whole family with their strange guests sat down shortly to a bountiful supper.

"The more you eat the better I shall like it," said Thor, as they took their places at the table, "but do not on any account break the bones; when you have done with them throw them into the skins which I have spread out on the hearth."

The peasant and his wife and Thjalfe and Roskva, their two children, ate bountifully; but Thjalfe broke one of the bones to get the marrow. Thor did not notice this.

The next morning Thor was up with the sun, and when he had dressed himself he took the hammer and held it over the goat-skins: and immediately the bones flew into place, and the skins covered them, and there were the two goats as full of life as when they started out the day before.

But one of the goats limped; and when Thor saw it he was so angry that he looked like a thunder-cloud, and his fingers closed so tightly round Mjolner that his knuckles were white. Thjalfe, who had been looking with the rest of the family in speechless wonder, was frightened half out of his wits when he saw Thor's rage, and would have run away if he could. The poor peasant and his wife were equally terrified, and besought Thor that he would not destroy them.

Seeing them in such misery Thor's anger died out, and he said he would forgive them, but Thjalfe and Roskva must henceforth be his servants. So taking the two children, and leaving the goats with their parents for safe keeping, Thor and Loki set out again.

Thor had decided to go to Jotunheim, and all the morning they travelled eastwards until they reached the shore of the sea. They crossed the wide waters quickly and climbed up in the further shore of Jotunheim. Mists floated over the land, and great rocks rose along the coast so stern and black from the wash of the sea and the fury of storms that they seemed like strong giants guarding their country against the giant-queller.

Thor led the way, and they soon entered a deep forest through which they travelled until nightfall, Thjalfe, who was very fleet of foot, carrying the sack of provisions. As night came on they looked about for shelter, and came upon an immense building with a whole side opening into a great room, off which they found five smaller rooms. This was just what they wanted, although they could not imagine why anyone had built such a house in that lonely place. After supper, weary with the long journey, they were soon in a deep sleep.

Three or four hours went by quietly enough, but about midnight they were suddenly awakened by an awful uproar, which shook the building to its foundations and made the whole earth tremble. Thor called the others and told them to go into

121

the further rooms. Half-dead with fright they did so, but Thor stretched himself, hammer in hand, at the wide entrance.

As soon as there was light enough to see about him Thor went into the woods, and had gone but a little way when he came upon an enormous giant, fast asleep, and snoring so loudly that the very trees shook around him. Thor quickly buckled on his belt of strength, and had no sooner done so than the giant awoke and sprang to his feet. The whole earth shook under him, and he towered as far over Thor as a great oak does over the fern that grows at its foot. Thor was not frightened, but he had never heard of such a giant before and he looked at him with honest surprise.

"Who are you?" he said, after looking up to the great face a minute.

"I am Skrymer," answered the giant, "but I don't need to ask your name. You are Thor. But what have you done with my glove?"

And stretching out his great hand the giant picked up his glove—which was nothing less than the building Thor and the others had spent the night in!

"Would you like to have me travel with you?" continued the giant.

"Certainly," said Thor, although it was plainly to be seen that neither Thjalfe nor Roskva wanted such a companion. Skrymer thereupon untied his sack and took out his breakfast, and the others followed his example, taking care, however, to put a comfortable distance between themselves and their dangerous fellow-traveller. After breakfast Skrymer proposed that they should put all their provisions into one bag, to which Thor consented, and they started off, the giant tramping on ahead, and carrying the sack on his broad back.

All day long he walked steadily on, taking such tremendous strides that the others could hardly keep up with him. When night came he stopped under a great oak.

"There," said he, throwing down the sack; "take that and get some supper; I am going to sleep."

The words were hardly out of his mouth before he began to snore as loudly as the night before. Thor took the sack, but the harder he tried to loosen the string the tighter it drew, and with all his strength he could not untie a single knot. Finding he could not get into the sack, and hearing the giant snore so peacefully at his side, Thor's anger blazed out, and grasping the hammer he struck the giant full on the head. Skrymer opened his eyes drowsily.

"Did a leaf fall on my head?" he called out sleepily, without getting up. "Have you had your supper yet, and are you going to bed?"

In a minute he was snoring again. Thor went and lay down under another oak; but at midnight the giant began to snore so heavily that the forest resounded with the noise. Thor was fairly beside himself with rage, and swinging his hammer struck Skrymer such a tremendous blow that the hammer sank to the handle in his head. The giant opened his eyes and sat up.

"What is the matter now?" he called out. "Did an acorn fall on my head? How are you getting on, Thor?"

"Oh, I am just awake," said Thor, stepping back quickly. "It is only midnight, and we may sleep awhile longer."

Thor watched until the giant had fallen asleep again, and just at daybreak dealt him the most terrible blow that he had ever given with the hammer. It buried itself out of sight in Skrymer's forehead. The giant sprang to his feet and began to stroke his beard.

"Are there any birds up there?" he asked, looking into the oak. "I thought a feather dropped on my head. Are you awake, Thor? It is full time to dress, and you are near the end of your journey. The city of Utgard is not far off."

123

"I heard you whispering together that I was a man of great stature, but you will find much larger men in Utgard. Take my advice, when you get there don't boast very much, for they will not take boasting from such little fellows as you are. You would do well to turn back and go home while you have a chance; but if you will go on, take the road to the eastward,—my way takes me to the north."

Then, swinging the sack of provisions over his shoulder, Skrymer plunged into the forest and was soon out of sight.

Thor and his companions pushed on as fast as they could until noon, when suddenly a great city rose before them, on a vast plain, the walls of which were so high that they had to lean back as far as they could to see the top. A great gate, heavily barred, stopped them at the entrance; but they crept between the bars. After going a little distance they came upon a palace, and the doors being open went in, and found themselves in a great hall with long seats on either side, and on these seats rows of gigantic men larger than Skrymer.

When they saw Utgard-Loki, who was the king of that country, they saluted him; but he sat for a long time without taking any notice of them. At last, smiling contemptuously, he said: "It is tiresome for travellers to be asked about a long journey; but if I am not mistaken this little fellow is Thor ... Perhaps, however, you are really larger than you seem to be. What feats of strength can you show us? No one is permitted to stay here unless he excels in some difficult thing."

Hearing these words, in a very insulting tone, Loki answered loudly, "There is one feat in which no one can equal me, and I am ready to perform it at once. I can devour food faster than anyone here."

"Truly, that would be a feat if you could do it," said the scornful king; and he called to a man named Logi to contend with Loki.

A great trough full of meat was placed in the centre of the hall, and commencing at either end the contestants began to eat voraciously, and so fast that it is disagreeable even to think of it. They reached the middle of the trough at exactly the same moment; but Loki had eaten only the meat, while Logi had devoured meat, bones, trough and all. There was nothing left on his side, and Loki had to confess himself beaten.

Then the king, looking at Thjalfe, asked, "What can you do, young man?"

"I will run a race with anyone you will select," answered Thjalfe promptly.

"If you can outrun anyone I can select, it will certainly be a splendid feat," said Utgard-Loki; "but you must be very swift-footed to do it."

There was a noble race-ground just outside the palace, and everyone hurried out to see the race. The king called a slender young fellow named Hugi, and told him to run with Thjalfe.

There was never such running since the world began. Thjalfe ran like the wind; but Hugi reached the goal first, and turned about to meet Thjalfe as he came breathless to the post.

"You must use your legs better than that if you intend to win," said the king, as Thjalfe walked back; "although you are the fastest runner that has ever come here."

They ran a second time, but when Hugi reached the goal and turned around, Thjalfe was a full bow-shot behind.

"Well run!" shouted Utgard-Loki; "well run! a third race shall decide it."

A third time they were at the starting-place and again they were speeding down the course, while everybody strained his eyes to look at them; and a third time Hugi reached the goal and turned to find Thjalfe not half-way.

"We have had racing enough!" cried the giants, and they all went back into the palace again.

And now it was Thor's turn to show his wonderful strength; but he did not dream that he was going to measure strength with the most tremendous forces in the whole earth.

"Your fame fills all the worlds, Thor," called out Utgard-Loki, when they had seated themselves on the benches along the great hall; "give us some proof of your wonderful power."

Thor never waited to be asked a second time.

"I will contend in drinking with anyone you may select," was his prompt acceptance of the challenge.

"Well answered," said the king. "Bring out the great horn."

A giant went out, and speedily came back bearing a very deep horn, which the king said his men were compelled to empty as a punishment.

"A good drinker will empty that horn at a single draught," said Utgard-Loki, as it was filled and handed to Thor; "a few men need to drink twice, but only a milksop needs a third pull at it."

Thor thought the horn not over-large although very long, and as he was very thirsty he put it to his lips without further ado, and drank so long and deep that he thought it certainly must be empty, but when he set the horn down and looked into it he was astonished to find that the liquor rose almost as high as when he set his lips to it.

"That was fairly well drunk," said the king, "but not unusually so; if anybody had told me Thor could do no better than that I would not have believed him. But of course you will finish it at a second draught."

Thor said nothing, although he was very angry, but setting the horn to his lips a second time he drank longer and deeper than before. When he had stopped to take breath, and looked at it again, he had drunk less than the first time.

"How now, Thor," cried Utgard-Loki, "you have left more for the third draught than you can manage. If there are no other feats which you can perform better than this you must not expect to be considered as great here as among the gods."

Thor became very angry when he heard these words, and seizing the horn he drank deep, fast, and furiously until he thought it certainly must be empty; but when he looked into it the liquor had fallen so little that he could hardly see the difference; and he handed it to the cupbearer, and would drink no more.

"It is plain," spoke up the king in a very insulting tone, "that you are not so strong as we thought you were; you cannot succeed in this strife, certainly; will you try something else?"

"I will certainly try something else," said Thor, who could not understand why he had failed to drain the horn; "but I am sure that even among the gods such draughts would not be counted small. What game do you propose now?"

"Oh, a very easy one," replied the king, "which my youngsters here make nothing of; simply to lift a cat from the floor. I should not think of asking you to try it if I did not see that you are much less of a man than I have always supposed."

He had no sooner said this than a large grey cat ran out into the hall. Thor put his hand under it and tried to lift it, but the cat arched its back as high as Thor stretched his hands, and, do his best, he could only get one foot off the floor.

"It is just as I expected," cried Utgard-Loki in a loud voice; "the cat is very large, and Thor is a very little fellow compared with the rest of us."

Thor's eyes flashed fire. "Little as I am," he shouted, "I challlenge any of you to wrestle with me."

Utgard-Loki looked up and down the benches as if he would call out some one from the two rows of giants. Then shook his head, saying; "There is no one here who would not think it child's play to wrestle with you; but let someone call in Ellie, my old nurse; she shall try her strength with you. She has brought many a stronger man than you to earth."

An old woman came creeping into the hall, bent, wrinkled, and toothless, Thor seized her, but the tighter his grasp became the firmer she stood. Her thin arms gripped like a vice, her strength seemed to grow as she put it forth, and at last after a hard struggle, in which Thor strained every muscle to the breaking point, he sank on one knee.

"That is enough," said Utgard-Loki, and the old woman crept feebly out of the hall, leaving Thor stunned and bewildered in the midst of the silent giants. There were no more trials of strength, and Thor and his companions were generously feasted after their defeats.

The next morning, after they had partaken of a bountiful breakfast of meat and drink, they started on their journey homeward. Utgard-Loki went with them as far as the gate of the city, where he stopped.

"How do you think your journey has turned out?" he asked Thor; "and have you met any men stronger than yourself?"

"I have brought shame upon myself," answered Thor frankly and honestly, after his nature, "and it vexes me to think that you will hereafter speak of me as a weak fellow."

"Now that you are out of the city I will tell you the truth about these things," said Utgard-Loki. "If I had known how mighty you are I would never have allowed you to enter the gates, and you may be sure you will never get in a second time. I have beaten you by deception, not by strength. I have been deluding you from the start. In the forest I tied the sack with a tough iron wire in such a way you could not discern the secret of the knot. Thrice you struck at me with your hammer, and the first blow, though the lightest, would have killed me had it fallen on me; but each time I slipped a mountain between myself and the hammer, and the blows made three deep clefts in its stony sides. I have deluded you, too, in all the trials of strength and skill. Loki was very hungry, and ate voraciously, but he contended against fire itself, which goes like the wind and devours everything in its path; Thjalfe ran as man never ran before, but Hugi, who raced with him, was no other than my thought, and what man is so swift as thought? The horn which you strove in vain to empty had its further end in the sea, and so mighty were your draughts that over the wide sea the waters have sunk to the ebb. Your strength was no less wonderful when you lifted the cat; when we saw one foot raised from the floor our hearts sank in terror, for it was the Midgard-serpent, encircling the whole earth, which you really contended against, and you held it aloft so near heaven that the world was hardly enclosed by its folds. Most marvellous of all was the wrestling with Ellie, who was none other than old age itself, who sooner or later must bring all things to the ground. We must part, I hope never to meet again; for I can only defend myself against you by spells of magic such as these."

Thor was so enraged when he heard these words that he swung his hammer high in air to crush the lying Utgard-Loki, but he had vanished, and when Thor turned to look for the city he saw only a beautiful plain spreading its blossoming meadows to the far mountains; and he went thoughtfully back to Asgard.

The Giant and his Swing

From the Fiji Islands

By A. W. Reed and Inez Hames

Every country has its own legends to explain the existence of large boulders and rocks. Usually a giant is deemed responsible—even in the Fiji Islands, where a rather endearing giant called Bulai comes to grief on his swing!

In a tiny village in Naceva, far away in the mountains of the island of Kadavu, lived the family of Bulai. They were ordinary, hard-working people, but Bulai, the youngest member of the family, was a giant who had left home at an early age to live on the tops of the mountains.

Bulai was much fonder of play than work. He made enormous swings for himself from strong forest vines. They hung from the trees, and Bulai sat on the seat of his favourite swing at the end of a long creeper that hung from the biggest tree in the mountains.

With one gigantic swing he could fly across the mountains and valleys for twenty miles until he came to Nabukelevu; back would go the swing, right across the island, until he was far over the sea at the other end of Kadavu.

All day long the swing went backwards and forwards, and in its passage Bulai swung right over his own village. Every time he swung past he could see his father and the women of the family at work. At one time they were climbing up a track in the forest to the yam gardens; the next time digging yams with sharp pointed sticks. Another time they would be climbing the coconut

130

trees and cutting big leaves, while others sat on the ground plaiting the leaves into baskets.

Another swing and Bulai saw them putting the yams into the basket, taking strong poles which they placed over their shoulders, and carrying the heavy baskets home. Back went the swing again, and he could see them slipping and sliding in the mud up and down the hills, back to their own village.

As the swing went by in the evening he could see the women gathering firewood and carrying it to their home and, when it was almost too dark to see, the first flickering of the fires that were lit to roast the yams.

At that moment Bulai would stretch out his hand and snatch the roasted yams away from his family just as they were ready to eat them.

They were good-natured people, and at first, although they grumbled about it, they just went out and got more yams. But as day after day went by and Bulai snatched all their food as his swing hurtled over the village, they knew that something would have to be done about it. They shouted at him, but Bulai just laughed and took no notice.

One day two men went out of the village carrying stone axes. They climbed far up the hills until they came to the top, to the tree from which the giant swing was hanging. Up the tree they went until they could see right across the island and far out to sea. Below them was the creeper that Bulai used for a swing. They chopped at it until it parted; as it fell it coiled up in the valley far below like a snake, with Bulai entangled in it. He was killed instantly.

In a village somewhere in Naceva there are some large white stones which look like the bones of a giant. The people call them Bulai's Bones, and every time they look at them they say: "Those who think only of pleasure and leave all the work to others will come to a bad end!"

The Giant and the Pygmies

By Roger Lancelyn Green

In Ancient Greece the gods were all-important: they reigned in the upper air or on mountain tops, especially that of Mount Olympus, coming down to earth sometimes in disguise to rule the lives of men. There were many gods, each responsible for a different part of the earth. Zeus, the most powerful, was the god of thunder and lightning.

There were also many heroes, such as Heracles, who probably had historical origins, but whose miraculous and superhuman actions were so woven into the tales of the gods that we can no longer tell what was true and what was invented.

Heracles, the son of Zeus, was one of the most celebrated of all the Greek heroes, noted for his strength, courage and endurance. He was tricked into killing his wife and children, and overcome with remorse consulted the oracle at Delphi to see how he might be purified of his crime.

Heracles was told to go and serve the king, Eurystheus, and perform all the feats which the king commanded him. One of these "Labours of Heracles" was to bring back three golden apples from the Garden of the Hesperides on Mount Atlas. Heracles asked the Giant Atlas to get them for him while he held up the sky.

When Heracles had tricked Atlas into taking back his burden of the sky, he put the three golden apples from the Garden of the Hesperides carefully away in his wallet, slung it over his shoulder, and set out on his long journey back to Greece.

Instead of going across the desert from oasis to oasis and passing through Upper Egypt or Ethiopia—which might be dangerous after his treatment of Busiris and Emathion—he made his way along the sea coast of Libya, which we now call North Africa.

133

Even so, he met with several adventures on the way, the first being with a giant called Antaeus who challenged all who passed through his country to a wrestling match. And he was so strong that he killed all comers, and used their bones to thatch the roof of his palace.

Antaeus was not very much taller than Heracles, but he was broader across the shoulders than any man living, and his arms, right to the wrists, were as thick as they were at his shoulders. His great muscles stood out like ropes of iron, and he glared about him under his shaggy brows like some wild beast, while his body was tanned almost black by the sun.

"Ho, stranger!" roared Antaeus, when he saw Heracles striding towards him. "None passes this way without trying a fall with me!"

"Willingly!" cried Heracles. "I love nothing so much as a wrestling match, and I think we make a good pair!"

So saying, he unbuckled his belt, and flung off the lion skin which he always wore.

Antaeus crouched a little, his legs bent, his huge arms swinging, and advanced towards the fair-skinned Greek looking like nothing so much as a gorilla.

Before clinching with his adversary, Heracles rubbed olive oil all over his body, after the fashion of Greek athletes. He was surprised to see that instead of oil, Antaeus rubbed himself with sand and dust from the ground.

For a little while the two champions circled around each other. Then with a shout of "Now for you, miserable human!" Antaeus sprang at Heracles, and the two grasped one another in their mighty arms and stood straining and swaying, striving each to throw the other to the ground and fall upon him.

Heracles found that he could just hold his own against Antaeus, but only just. The giant, however, was not in as good training as the hero, and very soon the sweat began to pour down his body, and his arms began to weaken, and his legs to tremble. With a shout of triumph, Heracles put out his strength, and flung Antaeus to the ground.

But scarcely had the giant measured his length on the earth, when he sprang to his feet, all trace of weariness gone, and leaped at Heracles again. Once more the wrestlers struggled and swayed, Heracles only just holding his own at first, but Antaeus growing gradually weaker.

When the sweat was again pouring from the giant's brow, and he was gasping for breath, Heracles flung him to the ground. But this time he fell with him, still holding him in his arms.

The moment Antaeus touched the earth, Heracles felt the flailing muscles grow taut again, the sweat dry suddenly on his body, the strength surge through him like a fierce wave of sea— and in a moment he was flung aside and the giant was on his feet once more.

"So!" cried Heracles grimly. "The earth gives you strength, does it?"

"She is my mother!" growled Antaeus. "Like Typhoon the terrible, I am one of the earth-born giants. So beware, little man, for very soon you will grow weary, and I shall fall upon you and break your ribs, bone by bone!"

"A little rib-breaking seems certainly to be necessary," said Heracles, and he seized Antaeus once more in his mighty arms.

But this time he caught him just above the waist, swung him off his feet, and held him under his arm, resting on his hip. Struggle though he might, Antaeus could not escape, nor cause Heracles to fall, and before long he began to grow weaker.

Then Heracles exerted all his strength and squeezed the breath out of Antaeus. One by one the giant's ribs snapped like sticks, while Heracles hugged him tighter and tighter, and at last bent him across his knee and broke his back.

Then at last he flung him to the ground. But it was too late for

135

Mother Earth to help her monstrous son. The cruel giant was dead.

As Heracles stood looking at the body of his foe, so weak from the fight that he could hardly stand up, there was a whirr of wings, and Hermes, the Messenger of Zeus, stood before him.

Heracles bent his head in salutation, and the Immortal said:

"Father Zeus has sent me from Olympus to place this crown of olive leaves on your head—the victor's token. He has seen your struggle with this evil giant, and he bids me tell you that he is pleased with all that you have done and are doing to free mankind from such evil monsters and pests as the Lion of Nemea and the Hydra of Lerna—and such wicked men as Busiris or this giant Antaeus.

"He also bids me lay one more task upon you—but it is one that you will perform gladly. Before you deliver the golden apples to Eurystheus, go once more to Prometheus on Caucasus, as you planned. And when you come to where he lies, smite off the iron chains that hold him, and set him free. He will ask you why you do this: say that it is by the command of Zeus, who repents of his cruelty, which was caused by fear. Say that Zeus frees him, and pardons him, asking nothing in return, but only to work as before to bring blessings upon the race of men."

Then Hermes placed the crown of olive leaves on the hero's head, and was gone with a whirr of his winged heels before Heracles could look up or speak a word in reply.

Leaving the body of Antaeus where it had fallen, Heracles walked forward on his way for a little distance, until he came to a shady grove of palm trees. And here, being utterly exhausted after his fight, he sank down in the cool shade and fell asleep.

This was a foolish thing to do, for he had many other enemies besides Antaeus, and in fact there was a whole race who lived nearby who looked upon the giant as their brother and their protector, and were eager to be revenged on Heracles.

Fortunately for him, however, these friends of the dead Antaeus were the Pygmies. They were a race of tiny men not more than five inches high, but fierce and brave, not afraid to attack even a giant if necessary.

The Pygmies lived underground, in a great dome covered with sand like an ant-hill. For the only enemies whom they feared and tried to avoid were the cranes who came flying to their land when the first rains of winter began to fall in Europe, and who caught and ate them whenever they could. Each spring, however, the Pygmies sallied forth, riding on mounts just the right size for them, and attacked the cranes' nests, breaking any eggs they could find and killing the young birds. And from these expeditions they brought back egg shells to decorate their dwellings, and feathers to use in making furnishings.

The Pygmies, in spite of their size, were good farmers, and grew corn which they stored in their underground dwellings. But as the corn was of the same size as in the rest of the world, they were forced to reap it with axes, felling each stalk as if it were a tree.

Now they collected their army, and their King, Pygmaeus, directed the operations against their sleeping enemy.

One regiment he sent to attack his left hand; and two companies of bowmen to disable his right, being stronger. More archers, and a company armed with slings laid seige to his feet, while King Pygmaeus himself led the advance against his head.

The attack on the head of Heracles took the form of fire to burn his hair, mattocks and pickaxes to undermine his eyes, a door to seal up his mouth, and blocks to stuff up his nose so that he should not be able to breathe when his head had been captured.

Suddenly Heracles woke, and sat up in surprise, Pygmies falling from him in every direction, with their ladders and weapons of war. For a moment he stared at them in amazement.

Then he let out a great roar of laughter which sent the rest of the Pygmies scurrying for safety, and rose to his feet, paying no attention to the flights of arrows which did him no more harm than burrs.

He hesitated for a little as to whether to catch a few of his strange enemies and carry them off to Eurystheus. But with a shrug of his shoulders he shook them out of his lionskin, flung it over his shoulder with his wallet and club, and set out once more, chuckling over his latest adventure.

When he came to Lower Egypt where a descendant of Epaphus, Io's son, was Pharaoh, he was welcomed more kindly than he had been by Busiris, and given a ship to carry him across the sea on his way to the Caucasus where he had to visit Prometheus once more.

The winds were contrary, which made the voyage so slow to begin with that by the time Heracles reached the island of Rhodes he was almost starving. So he tied up the ship under the great crag on which the town of Lindos stands, and leapt ashore in search of food.

Although excellent for vines and fig-trees, the soil of Rhodes is not good for corn, being very stony. But presently Heracles found an old labourer called Thiodamus ploughing with two oxen, and cursing every few minutes as the ploughshare caught on a stone.

"Old man!" cried Heracles. "I am almost starving after a long voyage. I beg you to give me food."

"You can look for it yourself," growled Thiodamus. "I am not going to give you anything. Nor am I going to stop ploughing for you or anyone."

"But I shall die of hunger if I do not have food soon!" exclaimed Heracles.

"Die then!" grunted Thiodamus. "It is of no interest to me."

"If you will not give or sell, I shall take!" shouted the starving hero, losing his temper. And in spite of the curses and cries of Thiodamus he seized one of the oxen, killed it, skinned it, and soon had it roasting over a fire.

Presently Heracles sat down to dinner. "Come and join me!" he shouted cheerfully to Thiodamus. But the old man just stood by and cursed him.

So Heracles set to work, and he was so hungry that he ate the whole ox and left nothing but the bones. And all the time he was eating, Thiodamus stood and cursed.

Then he got up and walked back to his ship, Thiodamus following him, and still cursing. And presently the furious old man added stones to his curses, but Heracles paid no attention.

When he was on his ship again, however, he turned suddenly to Thiodamus, who had been joined by many other Rhodians, and cried in a great voice:

"People of Lindos, listen to my words! I am Heracles, the son of Zeus, and the time will come when you worship me as a god, and pass down to your children the story of how I once visited your island. And every year before the harvest you will sacrifice an ox to me: but in memory of today, instead of prayers and words of praise, you will worship me with curses such as Thiodamus is using now!"

Northwards still sailed Heracles, and he came next to the island on which the body of Icarus was washed ashore. And there he met Daedalus and helped him to bury his son. Then, having given the island its new name of Icaria, he re-entered his ship, and sailed on, up into the Black Sea, and round the coast to the River Phasis which gave its name to the beautiful birds, the Pheasants, who dwelt on its shores.

Up this he went until he could sail no further. Then he left his ship and continued on foot, climbing even higher and higher until he came to the top of Caucasus. And there Prometheus, the Good Titan, lay chained to the rock. But the vulture preyed no more on his liver, for Heracles had shot it with one of his poisoned arrows on his former visit.

"Greetings, Heracles, son of Zeus!" said the great Titan. "How have you fared on your quest of the golden apples from the Garden at the World's End?"

Then Heracles told him of all his adventures, and also of the message which Hermes had given him.

"Zeus bids you set me free, as you wished to do when you slew the vulture," said Prometheus slowly. "Did he not bid you ask anything of me in return? The answer to a prophecy, for example?"

"I was bidden to say that he asks nothing of you," said Heracles. "He sets you free so that you may once again bring blessings upon mankind."

"It comes into my mind," said Prometheus slowly, "that Zeus is no longer the cruel tyrant who bound me here. My sufferings have borne fruit, for Zeus has been afraid all this time, knowing that I spoke the truth when I said that one day he would fall as Cronos fell—and that only I could tell him how to avoid his doom. Zeus has learnt by suffering and is now a just and merciful Father of god and men. And now that he has set me free asking no reward but simply as an act of mercy, I will tell him, when the time comes, how to avoid his fate.

"Now, hero Heracles, strike off these fetters which have held me here so long in the service of mankind. And in memory of them let men wear rings on their fingers henceforth."

So Heracles raised his club and set to work breaking the iron chains which bound Prometheus to the rock. When at last they were loosed, the Titan rose slowly to his feet and said:

"I thank you, son of Zeus. Go now and carry the golden apples to Eurystheus. But remember that I am not yet altogether free. I must go down into the Underworld where Hades is king and dwell there until you find a creature dwelling on the earth who is immortal, yet will give up his immortality and come to the realm of Hades to take my place. Let this be your quest, as you go on your way through life from labour to labour. For although you have only one more to perform for Eurystheus, all your life on earth will be spent doing labours for the good of mankind."

So saying, Prometheus passed down beneath the earth to dwell for a space among the dead.

But Heracles slung the wallet over his shoulder once more, and set out on the long journey towards Tiryns to deliver the golden apples of the Hesperides to King Eurystheus.

Finlay, the Giant Killer

A Scottish Story

By James McNeill

The Scottish hero Finlay was responsible for getting rid of the last family of giants in the country. And quite a hard time he had of it, for they were not only strong—but clever, too!

Long, long ago the Hebrides Islands off the coast of Scotland were over-run by giants. In time they were all killed or driven off by the courageous islanders, until only one family of giants remained. This family, which made its home in a long dark cave on a cliff that hung over the sea, was so rich, so cruel, and so crafty that the people of the islands lived in terror lest the giants come to rob and destroy their homes.

In these islands there lived a great hero and mighty hunter called Finlay the Changeling. He and his sister were the last of a family that had fought giants for hundreds of years.

Every day as Finlay left the house to go hunting with his dogs he would warn his sister, "Do not open the window to the north or let the fire go out." She always obeyed him and tended the hearth carefully; but one spring day she thought, "It is a lovely warm day! I will let the fire go out and open the windows to freshen the house."

In a little while she heard a soft knock. At the door stood a tall,

142

handsome youth, dressed in fine clothes. He had two dogs at his heels and the reins of his steed in his hand.

"I was hunting and lost my way," he said. "Would so fair a lass give a drink of cold water to a stranger?"

The girl was completely captivated by her visitor (who was really the younger son of the giant family and had been skilfully disguised by his crafty mother). She invited him in and they talked long and attentively. When he rose to leave, he asked if he could return again the next day.

"But you must not tell your brother," said the young man, "for I fear he would forbid it. Tomorrow I will wait on the high hill to the north. When the windows are opened and no smoke comes from the chimney, I shall know that I am welcome."

After that he came every day, for as soon as Finlay left, his sister raked the coals from the hearth and threw open the windows.

At last the young man confessed who he was. But Finlay's sister was in love. "I do not care *who* you are," she said, "I will follow you anywhere."

"Your brother will never allow you to marry me," the young giant replied. "But I love you so much I would kill him to have you. Let me tell you my plan."

That very day, as Finlay was coming home by the forest path, he happened upon a strange new dwelling.

"Good evening to you, Finlay Changeling," called a tiny, gnarled old woman from the open door. She had an immense shawl on her head and was winding a tangled mass of wool into a ball.

"Good evening, Grandmother," said Finlay. "Who are you and how is it I have never seen your house before?"

"I am called the Wise One," she answered, "and I have come to help you in your danger."

"I am the greatest hunter in the islands, my dogs are the

fleetest, my arrows the truest, and my sword the keenest. What danger could threaten me?"

"Your sister has fallen in love with the younger son of the giants. This very night she plots with him to take your life. When you go home you will find a bed of new rushes laid for you. Beneath the rushes lies the giant, who will strangle you as you sleep."

Finlay listened while the old woman told him what to do, thanked her, then set off for home, promising to return the next day.

His sister greeted him gaily at the door. "The soup is boiling above the fire, brother, and I have laid a bed of new rushes for you. Tie the dogs tightly and come to the table."

Instead, Finlay bade the dogs lie down in the corner, though they were growling and the hair was rising on their necks. "You are very thoughtful," he said to his sister. "Bring me a tub of cool water that I may wash my feet."

While the sister hastened to the well for a tub of water, Finlay carefully lifted the kettle of boiling soup from its hook. He threw the steaming liquid on the bed of new rushes, and the scalded giant leapt up with a shriek and ran screaming to the hills with his hands over his blinded eyes. Finlay's sister, seeing that she was undone, dropped the tub of water and, cursing her brother, ran after the giant.

Finlay's troubles had just begun. When the young giant reached home his family plotted revenge. His older brother wished to go himself but Laggan, the father of the giants, forbade it.

"A tricky enemy is Finlay the Changeling," said Laggan. "It will take wit to deal with him. I have five heads and they have kept me alive three hundred years. For the honour of the family I will go."

"Your five heads and my magic will work together," croaked

144

his wife. "Enough talking, I will prepare you to avenge our son."

That night, as darkness lay over the islands, Finlay sat alone before a roaring fire. His bow and sword were close at hand and his dogs lay restless at his feet. Neither the warmth of the fire nor the nearness of the dogs could dispel his foreboding.

"Fith, foth, there is a hindrance to hospitality in this house!" cried a voice suddenly. "The door is barred against the wandering stranger."

As Laggan began to tear the door from its hinges, Finlay seized his bow, climbed to the loft, and tore a hole in the thatched roof. Quickly he shot the eyes from two of the heads. Then he leaped down, sword in hand, as the door crashed in. The dogs attacked, and Finlay's sword swung quickly and deftly until the five heads were severed from the giant's shoulders.

In the morning Finlay twined the hair of the heads into a rope and went to see the Wise One.

"Well done, valiant hand. I see the father of the giants will kill no more."

"It was my brave dogs who made it possible," Finlay replied.

"There is yet need of them," the Wise One told him. "Tonight the elder son will come to avenge his father." And the old woman gave Finlay a handful of powder and told him what to do.

Finlay went home and spent the day digging a hole many feet deep in the centre of the cottage floor. Then he carefully laid thin boards over the hole. As night fell he waited with his dogs by the fire as before. Soon a rumbling like thunder sounded through the hills, boulder crashed against boulder, and tall trees snapped.

"Fi, foth, fugitive, the smell of an enemy is within these walls!" the giant shouted in the night, and the house trembled as he pushed the door in. Finlay cowered on the far side of the room, pretending to be badly frightened.

The giant stooped low to enter. Then with a crash his mighty form fell through the thin boards and he bellowed with rage!

Up leaped Finlay and threw the powder that the Wise One had given him full in the giant's face. As the giant's huge hands rubbed his stinging eyes, the dogs seized his ears and hair and held him fast while Finlay slew him.

In the morning Finlay took the massive head to the Wise One.

"Well done again, valiant hand, though your danger is greater than ever now. The great grey Cailleach, the mother of the giant clan, does not grieve for her family, for she has no tears. Instead, her anger grows hotter and her hate is boundless. She is strong and her trickery is unmatched. Stay here awhile and gather strength, for she will seek you out at the tide's turning."

So Finlay rested all day and drank a strong tea of herbs that the Wise One's daughter brewed for him.

Towards evening he returned home to prepare for the coming of the Cailleach. The night fell black and rain came with it. A tiny knock sounded at the door, so gentle that Finlay scarcely heard it above the beating rain. The dogs growled deep in their throats. The knock came again, louder this time.

Sword in hand, Finlay opened the door. Before him stood a little bent old woman, not four feet high, wearing a dripping cape made of chicken feathers.

"Is it Finlay the slayer of giants who welcomes me this rainy night?"

"I am Finlay. Come in, old woman. Sit by the fire and dry yourself."

The old woman sat at one end of the bench and Finlay at the other. Soon the dogs became restless and began to growl.

"Tie up your dogs, Finlay my son. I fear they will bite me."

"I have no cord to tie them with, old woman."

"Take this," she said, unwinding a long piece of red thread from the iron-grey hair that fell over her stooped shoulders. Finlay took the thread and, pretending to tie up the dogs, made them lie together in a corner without moving.

"Are the dogs tied?" asked the old woman.

"There they are in the corner," answered Finlay. The old woman looked at the dogs and saw that they were lying close together, and she smiled to herself, believing that they were tied with her magic thread.

"I see you are growing bigger, old woman," said Finlay.

"It is just the feathers of my cape drying."

"Your teeth are getting longer, old woman," said Finlay.

With a wild shriek the Cailleach sprang up and sank her sharp front fang deep into Finlay's shoulder. A mighty struggle followed. They fought in the cottage until the walls crumbled. They fought in the yard until it was a quagmire. They fought on the stony ground until the rocks were crushed into sand.

At last the dogs seized hold of the feather cape and pulled it from the Cailleach. Without it her strength began to fail, and despite his wounds Finlay pinned her down, breaking her arm and her rib.

"You are the victor, Finlay. Let me go and I will never bother you again."

"There is no truth in your words, O Cailleach."

"I will give you a trunk of gold and trunk of silver that are in my cave, Finlay."

"They are mine already, O Cailleach."

"I will give you a case of jewels that once belonged to fine lords and ladies."

"The jewels are mine already, O Cailleach."

"I will give you a gold-hilted sword that can overcome any man or beast on earth."

"The sword is mine already, O Cailleach."

"I will give you a magic wand," cried the old woman. "If you strike a stone pillar with it, the pillar will turn into a warrior. Strike the warrior again, and he will turn back into a pillar."

"The wand is mine already, O Cailleach."

The Cailleach was now very weak. Finlay let her go and the

dogs tore her to pieces.

In the morning Finlay took the tattered feather cloak to the Wise One.

"It is good to see you alive, valiant hand."

"I am alive and nothing more," replied Finlay.

"Rest here, and my daughter will heal your wounds with herbs and red moss," said the Wise One.

Towards evening Finlay set out for the giants' cave with the Wise One and her daughter. They gathered a load of heather and Finlay put it in the mouth of the cave. Just as the tide was coming in, he set fire to the heather and thick smoke filled the black cavern. Terrible were the curses and cries within the cave, and soon the blinded giant and Finlay's sister ran through the smoke and fell headlong into the sea.

That was the last of the giants in all Scotland.

"The treasures are yours, Finlay," said the Wise One. "But listen to me once more."

"Your advice has saved my life. I will accept it always."

"Take the trunk of gold and the trunk of silver for yourself, and return the case of jewels to the rightful owners. Anything that has magic in it cast into the sea."

"All this will I do, and gladly, O Wise One."

Finlay became a hero to the people of the Islands. With his gold and silver and the Wise One's daughter as his wife, he lived like a king for the rest of his days.

The Giant with Grey Feathers

A Canadian Indian Tale

By Cyrus Macmillan

The Canadian Indians passed down their history by word of mouth in the form of folktales. Mythical characters and events were used to portray what really happened, and giants always represented an evil threat of some kind. In this story giants are held responsible for the famine which has come to the plains of the Blackfeet Indians.

Once long ago, when the Blackfeet Indians dwelled on the Canadian plains, there was a great famine in all the land. For many months no buffaloes were killed, and there was no meat to be had at any price. One by one the old people dropped off because of a lack of food, and the young children died early because there was no nourishment, and there was great sorrow everywhere. Only the strong women and the stronger warriors remained alive, but even they gradually grew weaker because of the pinch of hunger visited on the land by famine. At last the Chief of the tribe prayed that the Great Chieftain of the Indians might come into his territory to tell the people what to do to save themselves.

The Great Chief was at that time far away in the south country where the warm winds were blowing and the flowers were blooming. But one night he heard the Chief's prayer borne to him on the winds, and he hastened northward, for he knew that his people on the plains were somehow in dire distress. Soon he arrived at the village of the hungry tribe. "Who has called me here?" he asked.

"It was I," answered the Chief. "My people are all starving because there are no buffaloes in the country, and if you had not come we should soon have all perished."

Then the Great Chief looked upon his people and he noticed that the old folks and the little children had disappeared; only a few children were left and they had pinched cheeks and sunken eyes. And he took pity on them and said, "There is a great thief not far distant. He is probably a wicked giant, and he has driven all the buffaloes away. But I will find him and soon you shall have food." And the people were all comforted, for they knew that the Great Chief would keep his word.

Then the Chief took with him the young Chief's son and set out on his quest. The people wanted to go with him, but he said, "No! We shall go alone. It is a dangerous duty, and it is better that, if need be, two should die in the attempt, than that all should perish."

They journeyed westwards across the prairies towards the Great Water in the West, and as they went, the youth prayed to the Sun and the Moon and the Morning Star to send them success. Soon they came to the rolling foothills covered with sweet grass and scrubby pine. But still they saw no signs of buffalo. At last they reached a narrow stream, on the bank of which they saw a house with smoke coming from the chimney.

"There is the cause of all our troubles," said the Chief. "In that house dwells the giant Buffalo-thief and his wife. They have driven all the animals from the prairies until not one is left. My magic power tells me it is so!" Then by his magic power he changed his companion into a sharp-pointed straight stick, while he himself took the shape of a dog, and they lay on the ground and waited.

151

Soon the giant and his wife and their little son came along. The boy patted the dog on the head, and said, "See what a nice dog I have found. He must be lost. May I take him home?"

His father said, "No, I do not like his looks. Do not touch him."

The boy cried bitterly, for he had long hoped for a dog of his own, and his mother pleaded for him so hard that at last the giant father said, "Oh, very well. Have your own way, but no good can come of it."

The woman picked up the stick and said, "I will take this nice straight stick along with me. I can dig roots with it to make medicine." So they all went to the giant's house, the giant frowning angrily, the woman carrying the stick, and the boy leading the dog.

The next morning the giant went out and soon came back with a fat young buffalo, all skinned and ready for cooking. They roasted it on a spit over the fire and had a good meal. The boy fed some meat to the dog, but his father, when he saw what the boy was doing, beat him soundly, and said, "Have I not told you the dog is an evil thing? You must not disobey me." But again the woman pleaded for her boy, and the dog was fed. That night when all the world was asleep, the dog and the stick changed back to their human form and had a good supper of what was left of the buffalo-meat. And the Chief said to the youth, "The giant is the Buffalo-thief who keeps the herds from coming to the prairies. It is useless to kill him until we have found where he has hidden them." So they changed back to the shapes of dog and stick and went to sleep.

The next morning the woman and her boy set off to the forest near the mountain, to gather berries and to dig up medicine roots. They took the dog and the stick with them. At noon, after they had worked for some time, they sat down to have their luncheon. The woman threw the stick down on the ground, and the boy let the dog run away among the shrubs. The dog wandered to the side of the mountain. There he found an opening like the mouth of a cave. Peering into the place he saw many buffaloes within, and he knew that at last he had found the hiding place of the giant's plunder. He went back to the woman and the boy and began to bark. This was the signal agreed on with his companion. The woman and her son thought he was barking at a bird, and they laughed at his capers as he jumped about. But he was in reality calling to his comrade. The stick understood the call and wiggled like a snake through the underbrush to the dog's side, unseen by the boy and his mother. They then entered the large cave in the side of the mountain, and there they found a great herd of buffaloes—all the buffaloes that had been driven from the prairies. The dog barked at them and snapped at their heels, and the stick beat them, and they began to drive them quickly out of the cavern and eastwards towards the plains. But they still kept the shape of dog and stick. When evening came, and it was time for the boy and his mother to go home, the boy searched for the dog and the woman looked for her stick, but they could not find them, and they had to go home without them.

Just as the woman and her son reached their house on the bank of the river, the giant-thief was coming home too. He chanced to look to the east, and there he saw, far away, many buffaloes running towards the foothills where the sweet grass grew. He was very angry, and he cried loudly to his son, "Where is the dog? Where is the dog?"

"I lost him in the underbrush," said the boy; "he chased a bird and did not come back."

"It was not a bird he chased," said the giant; "it was one of my buffaloes. I told you he was an evil thing and not to touch him, but you and your mother would have your way. Now my buffaloes are all gone." He gnashed his teeth in a great rage, and rushed off to the hidden cave to see if any buffaloes were left, crying as he went, "I will kill the dog if I find him."

When he reached the cave the Chief and the youth, still in the form of a dog and a stick, were just rounding up the last of the buffaloes. The giant rushed at them to kill the dog and to break the stick, but they sprang upon an old buffalo and hid in his long hair and, clinging on tightly, the dog bit the buffalo until the old animal plunged and roared and rushed from the cave, bearing the Chief and the youth concealed on his back. He galloped eastwards until he reached the herd far away on the prairie, leaving the giant far behind to make the best of his anger. Then the Chief and the brave youth took their old form of men, and in high spirits they drove the herd of buffaloes back to their hungry people waiting patiently on the plains.

The people were very pleased to see the Great Chief and the youth returning to the village with the great herd of fat buffaloes, for they knew now that the famine was ended. But as they drove the animals into a great fenced enclosure, a large grey bird flew over their heads and swooped down upon them and pecked at them with its bill, and tried to frighten them and drive them away. The Great Chief knew by his magic power that the grey bird was none other than the giant-thief who had stolen the buffaloes, and who had changed himself into a bird to fly across the prairies in pursuit of them. Then the Chief changed himself into an otter and lay down on the bank of the stream, pretending to be dead. The grey bird flew down upon him, for he thought he would have a good meal of fat otter. But the Chief seized him by the leg, and changing back to his own form, he bore him in triumph to his camp. He tied him up fast to the smoke-hole of his tent and made a great fire inside. The giant cried, "Spare me, spare me, and I shall never do you more harm."

But the Chief left him on the tent pole all night while the black smoke from the fire poured out around him. In the morning his feathers were all black. Then the Chief let him down. And he said, "You may go now, but you will never be able to resume your former shape. You will henceforth be a raven, a bird of ill-omen upon the earth, an outlaw and a brigand among the birds, despised among men because of your thefts. And you will always have to steal and to hunt hard for your food."

And to this day the feathers of the raven are black, and he is a bird of ill-omen upon the earth because of his encounter with the Great Chieftain long ago.

In the Orchard

By James Stephens

There was a giant by the Orchard Wall
Peeping about on this side and on that,
And feeling in the trees. He was as tall
As the big apple trees, and twice as fat:
His beard poked out, all bristly-black, and there
Were leaves and gorse and heather in his hair.

He held a blackthorn club in his right hand,
And plunged the other into every tree,
Searching for something—You could stand
Beside him and not reach up to his knee,
So big he was—I trembled lest he should
Come trampling, round-eyed, down to where I stood.

I tried to get away.—But, as I slid
Under a bush, he saw me, and he bent
Down deep at me, and said, *"Where is she hid?"*
I pointed over there, and off he went—

But, while he searched, I turned and simply flew
Round by the lilac bushes back to you.

**KANSAS CITY, KANSAS
PUBLIC SCHOOL LIBRARIES**

KCK-1